Essentials of Dyadic Interviewing

Qualitative Essentials

Series Editor:
Janice Morse, University of Utah

Series Editorial Board: H. Russell Bernard, Kathy Charmaz, D. Jean Clandinin, Juliet Corbin, Carmen de la Cuesta, John Engel, Sue E. Estroff, Jane Gilgun, Jeffrey C. Johnson, Carl Mitcham, Katja Mruck, Judith Preissle, Jean J. Schensul, Sally Thorne, John van Maanen, and Max van Manen

Qualitative Essentials is a book series providing a comprehensive but succinct overview of topics in qualitative inquiry. These books will fill an important niche in qualitative methods for students—and others new to the qualitative research—who require rapid but complete perspective on specific methods, strategies, and important topics. Written by leaders in qualitative inquiry, alone or in combination, these books are an excellent resource for instructors and students from all disciplines. Proposals for the series should be sent to the series editor at explore@lcoastpress.com.

Titles in this series:

Essentials of Dyadic Interviewing

David L. Morgan

Routledge
Taylor & Francis Group

LONDON AND NEW YORK

First published 2016 by Left Coast Press, Inc.

Published 2016 by Routledge
2 Park Square, Milton Park, Abingdon, Oxon OX14 4RN
711 Third Avenue, New York, NY 10017, USA

Routledge is an imprint of the Taylor & Francis Group, an informa business

Library of Congress Cataloging-in-Publication Data:

Morgan, David L. (Sociologist)
   Essentials of dyadic interviewing / David L Morgan.
      pages cm. — (Qualitative essentials; 13)
   Includes bibliographical references and index.
   ISBN 978-1-62958-361-7 (hardback) — ISBN 978-1-62958-362-4 (paperback) — ISBN 978-1-62958-363-1 (consumer eBook)
   1. Interviewing. 2. Interviews. 3. Dyadic analysis (Social sciences) I. Title.
   BF637.I5M67 2015
   158.3'9—dc23
                   2015017507

ISBN 978-1-62958-362-4 paperback
ISBN 978-1-62958-361-7 hardback

Contents

Thanks to

Jutta Attie

Paula Carder

Susan Eliot

Kim Hoffman

This book would not have happened without you.

1. Introducing Dyadic Interviews

The goal in dyadic interviews is to engage two participants in a conversation that provides the data for a research project. The broad outline for the content of such conversations—because they are interviews—is determined by the researcher's questions. At the same time, the goal is to provide the participants with a topic that will bring out their interest in what each other has to say. From the researcher's point of view, the conversations in dyadic interviews are the source of data, whereas from the participants' point of view these conversations are a chance to exchange ideas and experiences on a subject of mutual interest.

Traditionally, qualitative interviews have involved a single participant in one-to-one interviews or several participants in a focus group. There is thus an interesting gap in the size range, which does not include interviews that involve pairs of participants. Dyadic interviews fill that gap. However, given the naturalness of having two people talk to each other, it is not surprising that the equivalent of dyadic interviews has received some attention. In particular, two areas where such an equivalent has been used are marketing research and family studies. Within marketing research, focus groups have long been the dominant form of qualitative research (Greenbaum, 1998; Mariampolski, 2001). In this context, dyadic interviews are often referred to as mini- or microgroups. Greenbaum (1998) points to the value of dyadic interviews whenever the categories of participants come in natural pairs, such as partnered couples and buyers and sellers. Mariampolski (2001) highlights the use of dyadic interviews when recruiting the number of participants necessary for a focus group would be difficult or when a more in-depth discussion is preferred. Unfortunately, even though market researchers have promoted the potential value of dyadic interviews, there are very few examples of their use in this field.

By comparison, researchers in family studies (for example, Reczek, 2014) and related areas have made much more consistent use of dyadic interviews. The most obvious example in this field is the joint interview of partnered couples, although pairings of parents and children also occur. Similarly, there are studies that bring together pairs of friends and peers. In each of these cases, the defining characteristic is the use of preexisting relationships, whereby the research begins with an interest in some kind of naturally occurring dyad and then recruits sets of participants that satisfy this requirement. For present purposes, this approach amounts to a specialized form of dyadic interview, which is covered in Chapter 3. In contrast, rather than limiting dyadic interviews to preexisting relationships, this book uses a wider definition that includes the use of strangers who share an interest in a particular topic.

Dyadic Interviews in Practice

To illustrate the use of dyadic interviews, I rely on five examples of studies that have used this method (Morgan et al. 2013; Morgan et al., in press). The remainder of this introductory chapter summarizes each of these research projects.

The Experience of Early-Stage Dementia

Jutta Ataie studied people in the early stages of dementia to learn how their lives were changing after receiving this diagnosis. The primary interviewing technique that she used was photovoice (Wang & Burris, 1997), whereby the participants took photographs of the things that were important in their life and then discussed those pictures with the interviewer. Most of the data in the study consisted of individual interviews, but she also conducted a set of dyadic interviews that served in part as member checks (Lincoln & Guba, 1985) to learn the extent to which participants shared similar views with regard to her preliminary analyses.

Given both the special needs of this population and the sensitivity of the topic, Ataie chose dyadic interviews, which proved to be a good decision. In particular, pairing a participant with a similar person made it easier to create a sense of safety in exploring emotional issues. Further, participants' mutual understanding made it possible to overcome difficulties in communication and produce a lively conversation. As she noted, the participants "engaged in intense discussions that were characterized by sincere interest, respect, and curiosity, as well as a high level of interaction" (Morgan et al., 2013:1278). As the conversations progressed, the participants felt free to express diverging perspectives and even to disagree with each other, and this openness was quite useful in the member-checking portion of the interview.

Providing Informal Services to Elderly Residents of Low-Income Housing

Paula Carder studied a variety of social service workers who came in contact with elderly residents of government supported, low-income apartments. Technically, these residents were required to be living independently, but many of them received at least some informal assistance from social service personnel. By definition, this support was not coordinated, and these interviews were often the first chance that the participants had to meet others who had potentially comparable experiences. Thus these interviews were exploratory for both participants and the researcher.

The heterogeneity in these interviews was especially interesting, because the participants had encountered related issues from a diverse range of perspectives. In this case, the rare opportunity to compare similar and different experiences was more than enough to create active conversations in which participants often questioned each other in ways that triggered new discussion topics. This situation led to the expression of what was unique about each perspective as well as a sense of what was shared across the different circumstances that arose from the participants' different jobs.

Substance Abuse among Asian and Pacific Islanders

Kim Hoffman (Morgan et al., 2013) interviewed Asian and Pacific Islanders who were substance abusers, and they arranged additional interviews with pairs of counselors who worked with them. One of her concerns was her outsider status as a white researcher, so bringing together participants with shared concerns made it easier for them to discuss this sensitive topic. Further, her use of snowball sampling meant that many of these participants were acquaintances, which made it easy for them to create joint accounts and fill in each other's stories.

The results were, however, rather different in the interviews with the substance abuse counselors. In this case, the conversations produced useful data, but they were less lively and free flowing than the interviews with their clients. One major reason for this hesitancy was that the work turned out to be a sensitive topic for these participants, but not because of privacy concerns. Instead, the issue was that these counselors were universally white and thus experienced their own outsider status. In addition, there was a sense that the researcher, as an educated professional in their field, may have been judging their work performance. There was thus a reversal, whereby the participants who were most different from the researcher were most at ease, whereas similarities in status may have created a barrier to full participation.

Telephone Interviews with Physicians Making Changes in Their Practices

Susan Eliot conducted a study that evaluated a program to support rural physicians who were in the process of switching to a computer-based electronic medical records (EMR) system. Because the participants were both extremely busy and widely dispersed, she conducted the dyadic interviews by telephone. In choosing how to create the pairings, she wanted to have enough heterogeneity for the participants to compare their experiences, especially those who had more and those who had less experience with the EMR system. Throughout the study, she had assistance from a central member of the program itself, who served as a key informant with regard to issues such as which doctors would make good conversation partners, given that most of them were at least somewhat acquainted.

The most obvious implication for dyadic interviews was the success in conducting them by telephone. Because the study also included earlier rounds of individual telephone interviews with the same physicians, Eliot could draw conclusions about the similarities and differences between the two situations. Although the range of substantive topics was very similar, the dynamics of the interviews were quite different: the extended conversations in the dyadic interviews produced both more in-depth and broader data. In particular, the physicians were very interested in exploring each other's experiences with the sometimes difficult transition to EMR systems. This shared interest made it easy for the moderator to allow each interview to progress on its own terms, since the participants stayed on topic and required very little active prompting or probing.

Dyadic Interviews and Focus Groups with First Year Graduate Students

In my own work, I have done both dyadic interviews and focus groups with first-year graduate students, to hear about the experiences of becoming a graduate student. In both cases, the recruitment criteria specified that each participant should be from a different department or program. This requirement created a degree of difference between the participants and generated an interest in discovering what things they had in common and what was distinct. The result was a set of lively interviews in which the participants engaged in a great deal of "sharing and comparing" as they explored what had happened in the year since they entered graduate school. (See Appendix B for a complete transcript of a dyadic interview from this research project.)

Comparing the focus groups and the dyadic interviews showed that they both produced similar content, with the same topics appearing in each and receiving similar emphasis. Where the difference occurred was in the dynamics of the interaction. In the focus groups, each turn at talk tended to be longer and more self-contained, whereas the exchanges in the dyadic interviews were more rapid and intertwined. Note that these were typical examples of each format, rather than particularly "slow" focus groups or especially "energetic" dyadic interviews. Rather, these seem to be characteristic differences between group discussions and pairwise conversations.

2. Positioning Dyadic Interviews

Dyadic interviews have existed for some time under one label or another, including joint, peer, paired, an two-person interviews. Regardless of label, interviewing two people through their shared conversation is a general method that can be used for a wide range of purposes in qualitative research. This means that in many situations there will be a choice about when to use dyadic interviews as opposed to either individual interviews or focus groups. Often, all three forms of interviewing will provide a viable option, so the interviewer needs to have a sense of the specific advantages and disadvantages associated with dyadic interviewing. Hence, this chapter provides systematic comparisons of dyadic interviews with individual interviews and focus groups, respectively.

Before considering the comparison to either individual interviews or focus groups, we need to consider one other issue. The literature on focus groups typically treats four as the smallest number of participants, which means that three-person, or triadic, interviews have received just as little attention as dyadic interviews. This raises the question: why concentrate on just dyadic interviews? One obvious reason is that the classic idea of a conversation between two people is unique to dyads. Another reason is that the complexity of the interaction in groups rises rapidly with size. This complexity was famously discussed by Georg Simmel in his essay on the dyad and the triad.

As the figure on the next page shows, the two people in a dyad form a single, direct connection. By comparison, a triadic interview involves three connections between the participants. In addition, it introduces the possibility of indirect connections, whereby what one person says to another

Essentials of Dyadic Interviewing by David L. Morgan, 15–21 © 2016 Left Coast Press, Inc. All rights reserved.

Simmel on Dyads and Triads

Two-Person   Three-Person   Four-Person
Interview   Interview   Interview

must also take into account what the third person might think. The figure also shows the increasing complexity that accompanies larger sizes. The move up to four participants creates six possible connections. From this perspective, the interaction patterns among four participants do indeed look like focus groups, whereas the two-person interaction in dyadic interviews is clearly quite different. Whether triadic interviews also have something distinctive to offer remains an open question that is addressed in the final chapter on future directions.

Comparisons to Individual Interviews

The most obvious difference between dyadic and individual interviews is interaction. Of course, individual interviews involve interaction between the researcher and the participant, but this part of the process is not typically taken as part of the data itself. In contrast, the interaction between the participants in dyadic interviews is what produces the data. This fact points to the importance of the interviewer's role in both methods. In each case, it is the interviewer's job to ask the questions that determine the content of the interview, while taking either a more or less active part in directing the interview. In a one-to-one interview, the researcher's job is to make sure the participant provides useful data, whereas in a dyadic interview the goal is to get the pair of participants to converse in ways that generate useful data.

The difference in the interactive dynamics of these two kinds of interview is reflected in the concept of rapport (Rubin & Rubin, 2011). For individual interviews a feeling of rapport needs to be established between the interviewer and the participant, so that the participant feels comfortable talking about the research topic. In contrast, it is the rapport between the two participants that is crucial in dyadic interviews. It is still the researcher's job to do everything possible to establish this pairwise rapport, but that is a different task from working directly with one research participant at a time.

The issue of the dynamics between the interviewer and the participant(s), along with the dynamics between the participants in a dyadic interview, is also related to the topic of self-disclosure of sensitive topics. In individual interviews, the nature of the disclosure is directly to the interviewer, whereas dyadic interviews include the additional dimension of what the participants share with each other. Although there is no systematic research on whether individual or dyadic interviews would be a better match for topics that require self-disclosure, the literature on focus groups suggests that there are situations in which the chance to talk to *similar others* is especially effective in this regard.

For dyadic interviews, talking to similar others highlights the case in which a pair of people share a comparable background with regard to the sensitive topic in question, which allows them to understand each other's experiences in ways that an outsider might not. Examples of this situation from the introductory chapter include the studies on drug abuse among Asian and Pacific Islanders and on earlier stages of dementia, both of which involve experiences that require exchange of potentially discrediting self-disclosures. The opportunity to talk to someone who comes from an equivalent background can make it much easier to negotiate barriers involved in self-disclosure.

Interestingly, dyadic interviews may carry as much risk with regard to telling too much as too little. In particular, the participants in a dyadic interview may be encouraged to higher levels of self-disclosure by the rare opportunity to talk to someone who genuinely understands their circumstances. The extent to which the participants in a dyadic interview share something in common about the topic is the key factor, rather than any fundamental difference between individual and two-person interviews. Researchers thus need to move beyond the assumption that talking to another participant requires an additional level of disclosure, to a recognition that they may be just as likely to encounter over-disclosure

A separate category of differences between individual and dyadic interviews arises from the amount of time that two people share in a dyadic interview. When two people participate in a one-hour interview, the amount of information from each of them is essentially half of what would have been available through an individual interview of the same length. This means that dyadic interviews provide less depth and detail on each participant than a set of comparable individual interviews. The trade-off is that the interaction in dyadic information can elicit a process of sharing and comparing that engages the participants in discussing their similarities and differences; this process is discussed at more length in the chapter on interaction. For now, it is useful to point out that the greater range of topics explored in dyadic interviews can be an advantage that offsets the reduced levels of depth and detail obtained for each person.

Both the shorter amount of time available per participant and the nature of the interaction indicate that there are also likely to be differences in the kinds of narratives that are available from individual and dyadic interviews. In addition to the potential for longer, continuous sections of narrative, individual interviews provide the interviewer more ways to probe, either to extend a given line of narrative or to move things in a different direction. Alternatively, dyadic interviews are more likely to generate a dynamic whereby the participants "co-construct" a joint narrative. In this case, they are more likely to develop the subtleties of this progression themselves, although the moderator retains some ability to encourage or shift this process.

At the level of logistics, individual interviews are almost always easier to recruit and schedule. Putting together a dyadic interview requires not only locating two eligible participants rather than one but also finding a time when the two can meet. This means that 10 individual interviews are almost certain to be easier to schedule than assembling 20 people for 10 dyadic interviews. But this comparison also raises the question of whether it takes 10 dyadic interviews to yield as much data as 10 individual interviews. One possible way to investigate this issue is by comparing the number of interviews that it would take to reach data saturation, in the sense of generating no new codes (Guest, Bunce, & Johnson, 2006). In a rare direct comparison of focus groups and individual interviews, Coenen and associates (2012) found that it took five focus groups versus nine individual interviews to reach this form of data saturation. Unfortunately, Coenen and colleagues did not report the size of their focus groups, so the equivalent comparison between dyadic and individual interviews remains open to question.

Of course, it is certainly possible to combine dyadic and individual interviews within the same study. For studies that are primarily based on dyadic interviews, it could make sense to begin with a series of individual, key-informant interviews. The most likely use for such a design would be to learn from experts about factors that might affect the two-person interviews. An example would be issues related to pair composition, to learn what sorts of people would feel comfortable discussing the research topic with each other. Preliminary interviews with key informants could also help in writing the questions for dyadic interviews.

Individual interviews can also be useful for following up on dyadic interviews. One possible application for supplementary individual interviews would be to hear more from selected participants. In this approach, the original dyadic interviews would serve as a recruiting pool for a subsequent set of qualitative interviews, which would use the depth and detail of individual interviews to learn more from specific people. An example would be to learn more from people who had unusual experiences, or unusual responses to what were relatively common situation.

Another use for follow-up individual interviews would be member checking (Lincoln & Guba, 1985), where the goal is to hear from participants about the preliminary results from a research project. Thus, after conducting and analyzing the initial dyadic interviews, the next step would be to present those analyses and get feedback from the participants' perspective. These additional interviews could be done with people who had already participated in the earlier data collection or with new participants. In this case, the most obvious reason for shifting from dyadic to individual interviews would be the ease of recruitment, although the potential to hear similar messages from two different modes of interviewing could also be a motivation.

Comparisons to Focus Groups

Owing to the different kind of interaction that they promote, dyadic interviews are not just "miniature" focus groups. In particular the two-person *conversations* that occur in dyadic interviews are typically not the same as the *group discussions* that occur in focus groups. Typically, dyadic interviews produce a closer connection because each person is talking to just one partner, which gives the participants more opportunity to get to know each other.

One way to think about the greater closeness that emerges in dyadic interviews is through a simple comparison of the amount of time that the participants spend together. The basic comparison would be to a six-person focus group that lasted 90 minutes; in this common format, each participant would have an average of 15 minutes to speak. In contrast, a dyadic interview that lasted only an hour would provide twice that much time per person. From the researcher's point of view, this translates into an extended amount of data per person. The value of this extended data goes beyond the sheer amount that is heard from each participant because this conversational format also allows for more depth and detail as the participants respond to each other.

An important consequence of the increased depth in dyadic interviews is the greater possibility of conducting less structured interviews, in which the interviewer needs to exercise only minimal guidance over the interaction. This possibility applies to the comparison between dyadic interviews and both individual interviews and focus groups. Among the example studies, the one on physicians engaged in the process of adopting electronic health records included both an earlier round of individual interviews and a later round of dyadic interviews, which were both conducted by the same interviewer. In that case, the free-flowing conversations between the participants were a clear contrast to the more active probing that was necessary in the individual interviews. For the study of first-year graduate students, there were both dyadic interviews and focus groups. Once again, the interviewer found less need to play an active role in the dyadic interviews because the participants were almost always able to start and sustain their own conversation, given their shared interest in the research topic.

Aside from the interactive dynamics, the major difference between dyadic interviews and focus groups is the greater ease of scheduling and recruiting dyadic interviews. The key issue here is the difficulty of bringing participants together in the same place at the same time, and the sheer difference in size creates a straightforward advantage for dyadic interviews. This advantage is magnified when working with categories of participants who are either rare or hard to schedule. Putting together even small groups of participants can be particularly challenging in this situation, so working with only two people at a time can be distinctly preferable.

Another strength of dyadic interviews is a set of increased options for going beyond face-to-face meetings, by using tools such as the telephone, video, or online technology such as chat and instant messaging. Among these options, the one that has been explored in most detail is the use of the telephone, which was the basis for connecting the physicians in the electronic health records project. As that study illustrated, dyadic interviews

20

easily created the kind of person-to-person exchange that is the natural basis for telephone conversations. In comparison, the parallel possibility of conducting focus groups as telephone conference is likely to produce a much more formal kind of interaction. A similar possibility applies to conducting to video interviews in a format that matches the typical one-to-one conversation between participants. With regard to online interviewing, Morgan and Lobe (2011) point to the importance of maintaining small group sizes, owing to the complexities of "turn taking" when multiple people are typing their inputs at once; for those options, two people is probably an optimal size, because groups of four and larger have a strong tendency to become disorganized.

Finally, there is once again no reason to treat dyadic interviews and focus groups as competitive forms of data collection, because it is easy to envision research designs that combine the two. In particular, the possibility of following focus groups with dyadic interviews has a great deal of potential. This would involve picking interesting pairs of participants from the focus groups, so that those dyads could share and compare their perspectives in more depth and detail than they were able to do in their respective focus groups.

Conclusions

No one of these three kinds of interviews is more "natural" than another. In particular, whether the situation involves an exchange between the interviewer and one participant, a conversation between a pair of participants, or a discussion within a focus group, these are all instances of a very specific form of interaction: research interviews. Hence, it is best to think of the kinds of interactions involved in all three of these versions of interviewing as at most naturalistic, where each format mimics some element of everyday interaction at the same time that is reworked to meet the needs of the researcher.

In considering these three types of interviews as a set, one should recall that focus groups barely existed as an option in the social sciences before they were reintroduced in the 1980s. Until then, one-to-one interviews were the only available option. From the present perspective, the goal is to promote an equivalent position for dyadic interviews, where they can hopefully grow from a relatively unusual to a relatively common method for collecting qualitative data.

3. Relationship-Based Dyads

Within the literature on dyadic interviews, working with pairs of participants who share an ongoing relationship is an important option. Most of the work on dyadic interviews with previously acquainted participants comes from the literature on marriage and the family. The majority of the research in that field concerns heterosexual, married couples, with a smaller number of studies on parent-child pairings. The other notable group of studies involves friends, with a particular emphasis on adolescents and children. Between these two areas, the literature on marriage and the family is considerably more advanced with regard to methodological issues.

Dyadic Interviews with Married Couples

Dyadic interviews have been a prominent method among researchers on marriage and the family for at least 30 years, and many of the central issues were established in the earliest of these publications (for example, Allan, 1980). Probably the single most explored topic is the difference between interviewing family members (especially spouses) either together or separately. Fortunately, there is a substantial amount of consensus across the various treatments of this question (for instance, Allan, 1980; Arskey, 1996; Valentine, 1999; Eisikovits & Koren, 2010; Reczek, 2014).

Advantages of Dyadic Interviews with Couples, Compared to Separate Interviews

The most frequently listed advantage of dyadic interviewing is that the account it produces can be more complete, owing to iterative interaction. Among the specific mechanisms that have been noted in this regard are that in dyadic interviews:

- Participants supplement each other by adding details, remind each other about omitted material, and so on.
- Participants ask questions to make sure that points get clarified.
- Each participant helps the other person to express incomplete thoughts.
- The interviewer can observe whether and how a "division of labor" exists between the participants.
- Participants push beyond vague or conventional statements.
- Participants create more complex accounts by providing alternative versions.

The first three of these advantages relate to extending the content beyond what might have been available from participants answering the same questions in separate individual interviews. Processes such as supplementing statements, asking questions, and helping in general lead to the claim that accounts in dyadic interviews are likely to be more complete. Overall, these points give the impression of gentle, respectful responses to things one person has said, and these additional contributions are often positively acknowledged by the other partner.

Morris provides an example of this sort of interaction, between an older man who has cancer and his wife:

PATIENT: Well, I can tell you a little story, and it convinced the doctor that I wasn't worried about it. A few weeks ago, [*my wife*] bought this at the over-60s sale. [*Shows a small pot with a lid.*]

WIFE: Because I liked it.

RESEARCHER: You've got me intrigued now. [*laughs*]

PATIENT: Well, it is, it's a nice story.

WIFE: Because I liked it.

PATIENT: So when it came home, I said, "It's an urn." I said, "It's an urn, it has a lid on, you don't have that for flowers with a lid on." And of course she said, "No it isn't."

WIFE: He said, "You're a bit premature, aren't you?"

PATIENT: I said, "You're a bit premature, aren't you, that's an urn." Anyhow we laughed about it, which [shows] I really am not bothered. Anyhow, the week after they had the stall again, and she came home with a pot-type thing. I said, "What is that for?" "In case I can't get you all in there." So I told the doctor this story, and he just laughed, and he said, "You've convinced me you're not worried about it." (2001:xxx)

In contrast, when the participants are strangers, they have no opportunity to extend each other's stories; however, a similar process can occur in the joint development of topics within conversations between strangers. So, when a pair of participants who do not know each other can accomplish this kind of mutual encouragement, they are likely to reproduce the same advantages that occur in couple-based interviews. This is particularly likely in the case of question asking, which can also lead the first speaker to provide supplementary details or flesh out an incomplete account.

The other three advantages listed here support the common claim that dyadic interviews can produce richer data than separate sets of individual interviews. This richer data arises from processes such as when participants divide the labor in responding to interview questions, participants pushing each other to give stronger or more detailed statements, and discussing differences in perspectives or accounts. This kind of interactive work can be even more complex than the process just described. In particular, there is a possibility for disagreement, which can generate mutual resolution, congenial acceptances of differences, or even outright conflict. In interviews where the participants share a relationship, this conflict may represent well-understood aspects of the relationship, as illustrated in this passage from Bjornholt and Farsted:

MOTHER: Yeah, but that's not what the child needs. The child needs a routine.

FATHER: Yeah, yeah, yeah, we don't really agree ...

INTERVIEWER: Yeah, a little bit different focus in that sense, do you think?

MOTHER: Yeah, well me and the entire literature against him, I think ... Yes, children need a structured routine, it's just that simple, whether or not it suits you.

FATHER: Well, I'm ... I agree, but I mean our routine was overly ...

MOTHER: You just find it difficult that somebody else's routine dictates your day.

FATHER: Our routine was overly structured, but maybe it was what was needed because of his sleeping problems.

MOTHER: It took me eight months of really hard work to get that routine going, so it was really necessary not to ruin it. Because, if the daytime naps would change, then his whole night sleeping would have changed as well. (2014:9)

Returning to the comparison with dyadic interviews between strangers requires, once again, focusing on the work that those participants do to develop a shared topic. In this case, to the extent that there is a division of labor, the participants will engage in a series of interrelated exchanges, which may involve explicit negotiations over who takes the lead during any given part of the discussion. Pushing each other to say more or take stronger stands can also happen in interactions between strangers, although the norms of politeness in this context are likely to be different from those for married couples. The dynamics of disagreement are also likely to be different, with less need to produce a shared stance, and less likelihood of overt hostility. These general advantages occur through dyadic interviews, even though their exact form depends on the context that the participants bring to the interview.

Finally, another frequently mentioned advantage of dyadic interviews is the ability to use the interactions between the couple as a source of data. One observable aspect of interaction consists of attempts to support and influence each other. Like disagreement, this kind of interaction is likely to provide relatively overt statements that are easy for researchers to detect. A more subtle aspect of couples' dynamics involves how the participants create both individual and joint performances, as well as how they respond to each other's performances. Bjornholt and Farstad (2014) suggest "markers" in the interaction, such as laughter, soft or loud speaking, mumbling, and excited interjections. Even so, this potential advantage remains more of a hypothetical possibility for study rather than an active area of investigation.

Interactions between strangers are also likely to generate the opportunity to involve interaction during the co-construction of topics in their conversation. This co-construction may be more explicit when the participants are not acquainted, since that situation requires more active exploration of each other's perspectives. In addition, there is less possibility for coordinated performances based on mutual familiarity.

Disadvantages of Dyadic Interviews with Couples, Compared to Separate Interviews

Matching the potential advantages that dyadic interviews have over separate, individual interviews are two potentially important potential disadvantages. The first of these is the silencing and domination that can occur when one person controls the other's contributions to the conversation. These problematic interactive dynamics are by definition absent in individual interviews, since interviewing participants separately gives each an opportunity to produce his or her own account, without being directly influenced by the other. Even so, when uneven contributions occur in dyadic interviews, they may reflect individual styles more than couple-based dynamics, just as levels of engagement may also differ in individual interviews.

Compared to dyadic interviews with acquainted participants, interviews of two strangers are less likely to raise the issues of silencing and domination, but this kind of dynamic can still occur when differences in power exist. Hence, the chapter on group composition in dyadic interviews explicitly argues against bringing together pairs of participants when hierarchy is involved. In addition, the two chapters related to writing questions and moderating consider ways to draw both participants into the conversation.

The second disadvantage of dyadic interviews relates to desirability biases, such as a cultural emphasis on happy marriages, which both pushes interviews in that direction and creates the potential for embarrassment when this position cannot be maintained. In particular, conflicts that cannot be resolved can discredit the claim to have a successful or healthy relationship. The advantage of individual interviews is not only the possibility to minimize these kinds of cultural pressure but also to help participants to give different accounts without fear of contradiction. If there are problems in the relationship, the privacy of separate interviews should make it easier to admit to them. This advantage is, however, matched by a problem when the participants' accounts disagree; Hertz (1995) describes this as a "dilemma" in which the researcher must decide what to do about the divergent data. (The issue of disagreement also occurs in parent-child pairs, where it has received somewhat more attention, as noted in the next section.)

By comparison, interviewing participants who do not have an ongoing relationship eliminates most of these desirability pressures. Of course, both participants may be motivated to maintain a positive face with regard to some topics, which could lead to a tendency to accentuate the positive. Still, it is less clear whether this more general kind of desirability bias would be substantially exaggerated in dyadic interviews or alleviated in individual interviews.

Ultimately, the relative advantages and disadvantages of dyadic interviews and separate interviews with couples pose an empirical question. This issue is examined in some detail at the end of this chapter, after a section that considers variations in relationship-based interviews that go beyond married couples.

Dyadic Interviews with Parents and Children

Relationship-based interviews that bring together a parent and a child are also relatively common. These studies are, however, much less common than interviews with couples. In most of this work, the age of the child plays a substantial role; relatively few studies involve young children. However, Morantz, Rousseau, and Heymann (2012) did interviews among refugee families in which the target age range of the children was 7 to 18. In terms of working with adolescents, McCarthy, Holland, and Gilles (2003) interviewed both parents together but talked to each couple's teenage child separately, whereas Koenig Kellas (2005) studied triads with both parents and a college-age child. More common are studies such as Starkweather (2012) and Holmes, Bond, and Byrne (2012), which studied parents with a teenage child. In addition, Cronk, Gerkey, and Irons (2009) interviewed dyads that consisted of an older parent and an adult child. Of course, it would also be possible to include multiple siblings or even limit interviews to sibling pairs; no examples of these kinds of dyads were found, but Eggenberger and Nelms did conduct (2007) interviews with family members of all ages together.

One interesting feature of the literature on interviews with children and parents is that it has paid more explicit attention to the question of what happens when separate interviews produce different accounts. In particular, McCarthy, Holland, and Gilles (2003) ask if the problem of different accounts raises an issue about whether there is a "true" version of events or two different constructions of the same events. In some cases, this situation can be an interesting point of departure for more in-depth analyses, but in others it can create an irresolvable difference in the data. Ultimately, as Harden and associates note: "It was the task of the researchers to weave together the threads of individual accounts, their similarities, gaps, contradictions, and silences" (2010:448). This topic of agreement and disagreement will be revisited shortly.

Dyadic Interviews with Friends

Outside the literature on marriage and the family, there is a smaller research area that uses friendship as the basis for the relationship between the participants. Interestingly, almost all this work involves children and adolescents. Of course, there is no reason why dyadic interviews could not be used to study adult friendship pairs. For example, Galupo and St. John (2001) interviewed people in friendships in which one person was lesbian and the other heterosexual. Even so, younger participants make up the vast majority of work that uses friendships to create relationship-based dyadic interviews.

Interviews with Adolescents in Friendship Pairs

Highet provides a variety of useful methodological insights from his dyadic interviews with pairs of best friends on the topic of marijuana use. In particular, he argues that bringing together a pair of friends can create a "better balance in the relationship between interviewer and participants" (2003:111). In addition, he discusses the ways that talking with a friend can create a "safe context" to "both give and receive social support" (2003:114). Thus, compared to individual interviews in which teenagers may see an adult interviewer as an unwanted authority figure, interviewing peer-based pairs can shift the dynamic to a more comfortable one. This process is undoubtedly stronger between best friends, but it is not limited to those kinds of pairs. For example, Borland and Amos (2009) studied opinions about cigarette smoking among teens who were each allowed to choose his or her partner for the interview.

Highet notes that diminishing the role of the adult interviewer and maximizing the interaction between the friends can be especially useful for sensitive topics such as marijuana use. In particular, conversations between friends "may encourage young people to develop their narratives beyond well-rehearsed 'public' accounts'" (2003:114). In addition, as with couple-based interviews, peers who know each other well can use their shared history as a basis for monitoring aspects of self-disclosure—sharing what they feel comfortable revealing and otherwise maintaining each other's privacy.

Interviews with Younger Children in Friendship Pairs

Research on children in the 6 to12-year-old age range also points to the importance of using friendship dyads to counteract unwanted effects from an adult interviewer (Jones, Mannino, & Green, 2010). In this case, meaningful interviews can be difficult to conduct if the child uses interaction with parents or teachers as the basis for their responses. Once again, giving children the chance to talk to each other tends to overcome this limitation.

The most common tactic for this kind of interview is to do it during after-school hours at the school. This approach not only utilizes a well-known environment but also emphasizes a setting that is relevant to the friendship. Although it is possible for teachers or parents to select friendship pairs, it may be preferable to let the children nominate their partners. Either way, the goal is to shift away from an adult-dominated form of interaction toward a more comfortable and familiar format.

Comparing Dyadic and Separate Individual Interviews in Relationship-Based Pairs

Throughout the literature, and especially regarding interviews that pair family members, a debate continues on doing true dyadic interviews or conducting separate individual interviews. Aside from speculation, how much difference does it make? Given the amount of attention devoted to this issue, it is somewhat surprising that so little empirical work has been done. But the sheer logistical difficulty of doing both a dyadic interview and two individual interviews indicates the most likely reason for the rarity of such studies. In addition, no matter how interesting this question might be from a methodological point of view, most substantive research questions can be adequately addressed by using either one technique or the other. Even so, there is a handful of studies that have examined differences between interviewing partners separately or together as a couple.

Valentine (1999) offers one of the more detailed comparisons of the advantages and disadvantages of the two interview formats, based on doing both dyadic and individual interviews with the same couples. Even though this report is rather abstract, with no sense of the extent to which the differences described arose from an actual analysis of the data, the topics raised are familiar. In dyadic interviews, the participants can both validate and challenge each other, and watching how partners in couples attempt to modify each other's accounts gives insights into how the dynamics of the relationship operate. These processes can be particularly useful when each participant offers explanations for why the two see things differently. Alternatively, interviewing participants separately can create anxiety about both the degree of agreement and the inability to respond to what the other person might be saying, leading to participants' worries that they will be judged as a bad or unsuccessful couple. Individual interviews also leave the interviewer with unresolved questions when the two participants' accounts differ. On the plus side, separate interviews can create insights into how couples operate outside the interview situation, especially in terms of the accounts that each person can offer about how he or she accommodates the other.

O'Rourke and Germino investigated heterosexual couples' accounts of decision making about the husband's experiences with prostate cancer. In the dyadic interviews, the couples "untangled" their opinions and experiences, and, "even when disagreement surfaced, couples were able to shrug off their differences" (2000:241). Differences emerged, however, in the subsequent individual interviews. In one instance, this situation involved wives acting as "supportive spouses" in the dyadic interviews in the same way that they had in the decision-making process itself. That is, they felt that the husbands should have priority about making the decision, because they were the ones with cancer, and so the wives did their best to follow this path in the decision making, even when they had different feelings. This approach carried through to the interviews, during which wives first portrayed themselves as in agreement with their husbands' decisions during the dyadic interview and then used the individual interviews to reveal their restraint in both the original decision-making process and the joint interview. In essence, the dyadic interviews mirrored the actual experiences of the couples, wherein the men made the decisions and the wives provided support, whereas the individual interviews shed light on both the disparities that the wives felt and the ways they managed instances of disagreement.

Other researchers have, however, reported little difference in their experiences with dyadic and individual interviews. For example, Cronk, Gerkey, and Irons (2009) interviewed dyads that consisted of older parents and their adult children, both separately and together, and found no substantial differences between what was said in either format. Using a different design, Morris (2001) studied patients who had cancer and their caregivers, interviewing one set of participants separately and another set in pairs (that is, they did only one type of interview or the other with each pair). Again, they found little difference in the content generated.

An unusual alternative to interviewing the same participants with both techniques comes from Seale and associates (2008), who used a large database of secondary qualitative studies. They began by locating 37 cases of research that used dyadic interviews on health-related topics, which they then matched to studies that used individual interviews to examine the same set of topics. Seale and colleagues concentrated on gender differences, using systematic counts and content analyses. In one instance, they found that dyadic interviews increased such differences: not surprisingly, women and men generated about the same amount of data in individual interviews, but, against the authors' expectations, women did more of the talking in dyadic interviews. In another instance, dyadic interviews reduced a difference, in that women in individual interviews were more likely to use "I" language and men were more likely to use "we" language, as opposed to no difference in the dyadic interviews. In addition, a number of other analyses found no gender differences between individual and dyadic interviews.

Overall, there is too little data to make a conclusive judgment about either the extent or nature of the differences between interviewing relationship-based pairs in dyads or separately. Most of the studies that conducted both sets of interviews produced essentially impressionistic results, while the most systematic study on the issue (Seale et al., 2008) used a "matching" design rather than conducting both types of interviews with the same set of participants. Even so, the collective outcome of these studies indicates that interviewing family members either together or separately does not produce strong evidence of large differences.

An obvious caveat is that this issue has generally been phrased in a generic, context-free fashion, in terms of broad statements about the expected differences between the two interview formats. A more useful approach would be to specify the kinds of topics that most probably would cause these differences. One likely assumption is that differences would most commonly occur with regard to sensitive topics, when privacy concerns would affect issues related to personal opinions, especially if they conflicted with the real or imagined views of one's partner. Yet, the studies reviewed here were largely based on health-related issues, including severe illnesses. So even a claim for increased differences in the case of sensitive topics apparently needs a more careful refinement.

Perhaps the most useful approach is to ask why the comparison between dyadic interviews and separate individual interviews has been phrased as an either/or issue. As the study by O'Rourke and Germino (2000) nicely illustrates, when one is working with role-based pairs individually or jointly, each method has its own advantages and disadvantages. In particular, these authors' goal of understanding shared decision-making points to the advantages of observing the co-construction process that occurs in dyadic interviews. Alternatively, an emphasis on how individual perspectives fit together points to the advantages of individual interviewing. The process of combining the two approaches is certain to remain rare because of the effort required, but, as this study illustrates, it can provide unique benefits.

Conclusions

The work on interviews that involve preexisting relationships undoubtedly constitutes the largest literature on dyadic interviews. Some of this work covers topics that are of interest to anyone doing dyadic interviews, such as the general advantages of doing interviews with pairs of participants. Other parts of it address issues that are unique to marriage and family, such as the difference between doing dyadic or separate interviews with spouse-partner pairs. Overall, it is probably best to view interviews with participants who share a relationship as a special case within the larger field of dyadic interviews. Thus, the broader research topic is likely to determine whether the participants do or do not share a relationship.

4. Ethical Issues

D yadic interviews pose the same ethical issues as does most social science research, including the need for informed consent and the importance of balancing risk and benefit. Where they present a less common set of challenges is with regard to confidentiality, because the two participants disclose information to each other. Although this lack of confidentiality applies to both dyadic interviews in general and relationship-based interviews in particular, it is particularly relevant in any situation in which the participants are engaged in an ongoing relationships. Hence, this chapter begins with a general overview of confidentiality in dyadic interviews, followed by a more specific treatment of relationship-based interviews.

Confidentiality in Dyadic Interviews

The same interaction that is at the heart of dyadic interviews is also the source of a major ethical issue: the researcher's inability to guarantee confidentiality to the participants. In the classic case in which research is reviewed by an external board, the researcher is responsible for protecting the identity of the participants so that no one outside the research team can determine who the participants were. In dyadic interviews, however, each participant automatically has access to everything the other person says. This makes it impossible to maintain confidentiality, because the researcher has no control over what the participants do after the interview is over. To both emphasize and clarify this point, the consent form should include a clause stating the necessity of not disclosing the content of what others have said in the interview. This same constraint also applies to focus groups, of course, and the longer history of this interviewing method has led to ways of stating the issue of possible *lack of confidentiality* as an explicit part of the informed consent form. Here is an example:

> Any information that is obtained in connection with this project will be kept confidential by the researcher, and any identifying information will be removed from the transcriptions of your discussion. However, confidentiality cannot be guaranteed in a group setting. Please respect one another's privacy by not repeating what was said at this meeting or who attended.

Although this kind of statement is adequate for the purposes of informed consent, it also makes sense to give the participants a more detailed description of this issue. Thus, the instructions for the interview can include a statement such as this:

> Each of you is responsible for protecting the privacy of the other partici- pant in this conversation. In the same way that you don't want that person to disclose confidential information about you, you also need to respect him or her by not repeating what that person says today. Even so, neither of you actually has control over what the other person does after the inter- view, and that means the most important way to protect your privacy is by not saying anything that you don't want other people to know. I'll also be monitoring that during the interview, and if I think you are getting into topics that are too personal, I'll redirect you back into some safer topics.

In cases where privacy is essential, there are special techniques that can be used to eliminate the participants' ability to identify each other. One is to let the participants choose pseudonyms for themselves as part of the recruitment process. This has the advantage of heightening awareness of issues related to confidentiality and disclosure at the beginning of the research process. Another possible strategy is to rely on telephone inter- views, which can be especially effective when the participants live relatively far apart, because neither of them is likely to come in contact with anyone who knows the other person.

Confidentiality in Relationship-Based Dyadic Interviews

Whenever the participants are family members or friends, the lack of con- fidentiality poses a unique issue that stems from the ongoing nature of the relationship. In this case, the things that participants say and hear in the interview can have continuing effects after the interview. These effects may go beyond confidentiality violation to other forms of risk. In particular, the things that happen in the interview can become a source of stress in the participants' lives. This possibility creates a clear requirement for the interviewer to plan ahead with regard to self-disclosure when both partners in a relationship are interviewed together. In particular, from an ethical point of view, this requirement may mean exercising a certain amount of care to allow the participants to "preserve face," rather than pushing for more intimate data.

One potential solution to these problems is to do separate interviews with the partners, rather than dyadic interviews; however, different versions of the same kind of trouble can occur when the interviews are done separately. In particular, the participants may talk to each other between the two interviews and will almost certainly compare notes afterward. The potential for lasting effects within an ongoing relationship is thus modified rather than eliminated when the participants are interviewed separately. Hence Bjornholt and Farstad (2012) argue in favor of dyadic interviews on ethical grounds, because the couple has joint control over what is and is not disclosed. One tactic that can help in this regard is to have the participants themselves work on a set of ground rules for the discussion. This kind of negotiation both increases awareness and helps the interviewer to understand the comfort level of the participants.

Conclusion

Ultimately, it is the researcher's job to make ethical decisions about what happens in any kind of study, and dyadic interviews are no different. Although it is certainly possible to make recommendations about issues such as confidentiality, every case is different and thus requires careful attention to anything that might put the research participants "at risk." This is more than just an issue of what will satisfy a review board; it is a matter of personal responsibility.

5. Interaction as the Foundation for Dyadic Interviews

Interaction creates the data in dyadic interviews and is thus absolutely essential to understanding this method. Still, "saying that the interaction in focus groups produces the data is not the same as saying that the interaction itself is the data" (Morgan, 2010:718), and the same goes for dyadic interviews. Some specific fields, such as Conversation Analysis, do quite literally take the talk in interviews as their data, and this topic receives more attention later in this chapter. Still, the vast majority of interview studies of all forms are primarily interested in the substantive content of what was said. Thus, the studies that serve as the examples for this book were *about* topics such as the lives of people in the early stages of dementia or the experiences of first-year graduate students.

This chapter describes both the nature of interaction in dyadic interviews and the underlying mechanisms that the participants use to create and maintain that interaction. Issues related to the researcher's role in creating and maintaining interaction are covered later, in the chapters on research design. Each of these inputs to the interactive process are important, but for now it will be enough to say that the participants play the indispensable part in their own conversation, and researchers need to keep this in mind to achieve the desired kinds of conversations in dyadic interviews.

Unfortunately, there are relatively few techniques for investigating the interaction that occurs in dyadic interviews. Instead, there is a continuing acknowledgment of the importance of interaction without an equivalent

Essentials of Dyadic Interviewing by David L. Morgan, 39–46 © 2016 Left Coast Press, Inc. All rights reserved.

development of methods to study it. Still, saying that there are few tools for examining interaction does not imply a complete absence, and the next two sections describe some of the available options.

Conversation Analysis as a Tool for Analyzing Interaction

Various forms of Conversation Analysis are one of the most frequent approaches to studying the interaction in focus groups (for example, Macnaghten & Myers, 1999; Puchta & Potter, 2004), and there is every reason to believe that these techniques are equally relevant for dyadic interviews. One of the primary tools in conversation analysis is the examination of "turn taking," which captures each person's response to what was said immediately before that (for instance, Halkier, 2010). While conversations by definition consist of statements and replies, concentrating on turn taking can easily lead to an analysis that is too micro-oriented to get at the ongoing process of interaction. Gronkjaer and associates (2011) offer a useful compromise by working with sequences of turns that constitute "events" within the interaction. One example of the kind of events they deal with is "negotiating and constructing normality" (2011:19), so that participants consider the range of behaviors that fit with their views of acceptable behavior. Another example is dealing with agreement and disagreement, which goes beyond adjacent pairs or statements that express the equivalent of "yes" or "no" responses to capture the broader exploration of the degree of consensus and its sources.

Another common feature of Conversation Analysis, as it has been applied to focus groups, is a concentration on interaction between the moderator and the participants. For instance, Puchta and Potter (2002) investigated how moderators helped "manufacture" opinions by getting participants to make statements that seemed as if they had stable free-standing beliefs that didn't depend on the nature of the situation or who the other participants were. Similarly, Myers (2007) considers the ways that moderators "shape" the participants' interaction. This emphasis on active moderating is, however, only one alternative for conducting focus groups. In particular, Morgan (1996) describes techniques that allow moderators to take a less directive approach by relying on the participants to maintain their own discussion.

Regardless of the version of Conversation Analysis that one considers, it is important to understand that all versions concentrate on the *microdynamics* of interaction. Concepts such as turn taking tend to examine how conversations are built one piece at a time. As noted at the beginning of this chapter, Conversation Analysis tends to study talk itself, with much less attention to what that talk is about. As an alternative, the next section presents an approach that uses the content of the conversation to study the dynamics of interaction.

The Co-Construction of Interaction in Dyadic Interviews

Interaction in dyadic interviews is not an automatic and self-sustaining process. Instead, it is co-constructed by the participants and guided by the moderator. As noted, the role of the moderator is considered in some detail in a later chapter, so here I highlight the ways that the participants themselves work together to assure the coherence of their ongoing conversation.

What do participants use as the raw material for constructing their conversations? It makes sense to argue that *topics* should be treated as the fundamental unit for tracking the interaction in focus groups and dyadic interviews. Thus, as each person responds to what the previous participant said, he or she needs to take into account the content of that statement. More often than not, there is no need to announce how what is currently being said connects to what was just said. When participants have a shared interest in a topic, most of their exchanges do not need explicit management in the form of statements that overtly connect what is being said now to what was just said. What is more likely to be explicit in dyadic interviews is recognition of the previous speaker's contribution to the conversation, including such comments as "That's a good point" or "I know what you mean." In essence, the subject matter of the discussion takes care of itself, while the participants use mutual acknowledgement to demonstrate their interest in what each other has to say.

Of course, there are occasions when participants do directly address how their input to the topic is connected to the content of the previous statement. Aside from participants' simply announcing a shift in topic, Morgan (2012) describes two major techniques for the co-construction interaction: sharing and comparing. Sharing thoughts with regard to the topic consists of making an addition to what was just said, such as "Another thing that goes with that ..." or "And that makes me think of...." Developing shared thoughts about the topic helps to *extend* the conversation in the same direction. Alternatively, comparing takes the topic in a new but related direction—for example, by saying "The other thing that can happen is …" or "I guess my experience is not quite the same.…" Comparing thoughts or experiences about the topic helps to *differentiate* the possible directions for the conversation. In combination, sharing and comparing provide a powerful set of tools that participants can use as the basis for working with the topics that make up their conversation.

Just because the interaction is co-constructed within the interview does not mean that this process is its starting point. Rather, the participants must enter the interview with an adequate set of shared understandings before they can conduct a conversation of any kind. One useful way of thinking about this is to determine the extent to which participants share common ground.

Common Ground as a Basis for Interaction

Hyden and Bulow (2003) introduced the idea of common ground as a key element for examining the interaction in focus groups. As the discussion proceeds, each participant's statements help the rest of the group to understand the things that they share from their background, which can easily serve as a basis for further conversation. Among the things that can contribute to common ground are shared vocabulary, mutual knowledge, and similar experiences. When the conversation in a dyadic interview reveals a high level of common ground, each participant can take a great deal for granted about the other and build on that to create a more complex understanding of the topic. Conversely, when it is difficult for participants to find common ground, their conversation is likely to be hesitant and potentially superficial.

Hyden and Bulow include a distinction between establishing common ground and adding to or expanding on common ground. Establishing common ground is essential during the early parts of the interview in order to generate a smooth series of exchanges between the participants. From a practical point of view, the establishment of common ground typically begins with decisions about the composition of the pairs, in terms of their connection to the research topic. As described in the chapter on pair composition, creating a successful conversation requires that the participants feel comfortable talking to each other about the research topic, so the decision about whom to bring together for the interview has to take into account the nature of the common ground that the participants will share. When the participants are contacted and recruited into the research, they will almost always be presented with a summary of how they fit into the research project through their relationship to the research topic. Because of the dyadic nature of the interview, each participant will typically be informed about how his or her partner relates to the topic. Thus, by the time the participants arrive at the interview, a certain degree of common ground will already have been established.

In terms of adding to or expanding on common ground during the ongoing discussion, the interview questions that make up the interview require essential consideration. As described in Chapter 7, the interview often begins with a brief get-acquainted question that helps to establish and reinforce the preexisting common ground. After that, the first major question that opens the discussion needs to take into account the process of building on that initial level of common ground. Rather than pushing directly into the research team's interests, this "conversation starter" question is often oriented to the participants' interests. Central to each participant's interests is finding out more about the other person and learning how his or her own feelings and experiences relate to what the other person has to say. Hence, thinking about how the early stages of the conversation can add to and expand the participants' common ground is essential to creating effective questions in dyadic interviews.

Common ground is a powerful way to think about the interaction in dyadic interviews, but the current work in this field goes only part of the way. In particular, the theoretical framework associated with common ground remains relatively underdeveloped. Although there is an emphasis on the basic ideas of establishing and adding to common ground, there is little attention to issues that go beyond this. As a consequence, the existing work tends to stop at a recognition of the importance of common ground, without providing a broader model. Fortunately, there is a related approach that moves in that direction

The Co-Construction of Meaning in Interaction

The concept of the co-construction of meaning through the interaction in focus groups was introduced by Wilkinson (1998a, 1998b) and has received considerable elaboration since then (Hyden & Bulow, 2003;

Lehoux, Poland, & Daudelin, 2006; Moen et al., 2010; Morgan, 2012). The basic idea is that the participants work together to define and elaborate on the topics of their conversation. This process occurs throughout a dyadic interview as the ideas that were expressed earlier become the subject for further discussions. The two participants thus build on what each other says to create a context that exercises an influence on both what is said in immediate responses to the other person's remarks and what is said later in the ongoing exchange between the participants.

This co-construction of meaning can be thought of as including Hyden and Bulow's concepts of establishing common ground and adding to or expanding common ground. In addition, it includes a more abstract process of creating common ground that goes beyond what the participants initially brought to the interview. In particular, differences (as opposed to similarities) can open up the opportunity to explore each other's point of view. For example, one of the graduate student focus groups included a participant who felt that her interests were much more practical and applied than those of most of the students in her program, in contrast to the other participant, who felt that her goals were more academically oriented than were the career-based motivations of most other students in her program. This clear difference in the participants' purposes for being in graduate school might seem to be a problematic lack of common ground. Instead, they co-constructed a shared point of view whereby they were each relatively deviant from the mainstream in their respective programs. The result was a lively and highly supportive conversation.

Note that this co-construction of meaning is rather different from the co-construction of interaction described earlier. When participants talk about the topics that serve as the basis for their interaction, this is what makes the co-creation of meaning possible. The topics that serve as a basis for the participants' interaction certainly have to have a shared meaning to the participants, or communication would be impossible. The co-construction of meaning involves a specific process, which can be thought of as the discovering of topics that are truly meaningful to the participants. Thus, the conversational discussion of topics that have mutual interest may or may not involve the co-creation of meaning. On the one hand, that kind of conversation often involves a rather straightforward exchange of views, but, on the other hand, it can occasionally spark a sense of genuine inspiration whereby participants feel they have generated insights that would not have been possible without their interaction.

Putting Interaction in Its Proper Place

This chapter has reviewed a number of different approaches to the study of interaction in dyadic interviews. At one extreme is Conversation Analysis, which offers highly developed techniques for analyzing the micro-dynamics of talk. At the other extreme, the co-construction of meaning offers intuitive insights without specific methods for pursuing them, and the same could be said about the creation of common ground. Somewhere in the middle, the co-construction of interaction approach relies on the topics of conversations to understand the dynamics of the interaction.

With all these options, one can easily lose sight of the fact that interaction is important, because it serves as the source of the data in dyadic interviews. As Morgan (2010) points out, the core goals for the vast majority of researchers are centered on *what* participants say, not on *how* they say it. As noted at several points, this means that interaction has to be about something and that something meets the needs of both the participants and the research team. For the participants, the ability to carry on a conversation requires a mutually relevant topic. For the researchers, obtaining useful data depends on getting the participants to talk about things that match the research goals. Producing meaningful interaction requires attention to both participants' and the researchers' interests.

Conclusions

It is essential to recognize that *the quality of the data in dyadic interviews depends on the quality of the interaction between the participants*. Hence, research design in dyadic interviews centers on creating conversations. Designing research is all about making choices, and in this case these are choices about how to generate the desired forms of interaction. The next three chapters address the fundamental decisions that go into research design for dyadic interviews: Who will the participants be? What will the interview questions be? How will the interviews be conducted? The answers to these questions require a *balance* between the needs of the participants and the needs of the researchers. Thus, as the research teams makes choices about who the participants will be, they need to consider not only who can provide the data they need but also whether these potential participants will be comfortable interacting with each other. Similarly, the subjects of the interview questions must go beyond the researchers' interests, so that the participants will find those topics sufficiently engaging. Finally, the moderator needs to guide the conversation in ways that assure its value to the research team, while also allowing the participants room to express themselves through their own conversations.

In the end, the participants' conversations in dyadic interviews are the researchers' data, but this reciprocity will not occur automatically. To create appropriate conversations, the research team must bring together participants who fit well with each other, then ask them questions that catch their interest while moderating in ways that prove an appropriate direction for the conversation. All these decisions mean that there is no one right way to do dyadic interviews. Instead, choosing among the available alternatives requires knowing what the options are and knowing how to evaluate those options, so that the final design is most likely to meet the research goals. The next three chapters provide the basis for these decisions.

6. Pair Composition in Dyadic Interviews

The first step in designing dyadic interviews is to determine who the participants will be. This decision comes first because other choices about which questions to ask or how to do the moderating depend on the goal of creating interaction between a specific set of participants. As noted in the previous chapter, selecting the types of participants who will make up the pairs in dyadic interviews requires attention to interaction. The underlying question in pairing participants is thus: what is the likely nature of the interaction between one type of participants and another?

The Central Importance of the Research Topic

The general principle of balancing the needs of the participants and the researchers means that there are two important considerations in selecting participants for dyadic interviews: how they relate to the interview topic and how they relate to each other. The combination of these two factors indicates how easily the two participants can interact with each other in the interview. Thus, the participants' conversation depends on how they feel about discussing this particular topic with this particular partner.

From the researcher's perspective, however, it is too easy to concentrate on topic-related considerations, with less attention to how the participants will relate to each other. This situation is only natural, because the topic determines the inclusion and exclusion criteria that define the purposive sampling strategy for the study. To the extent that participants meet the preferred criteria, the things they have to say are likely to serve the purposes of the project.

Even though sampling criteria for the study are essential, matching them is not enough. Obtaining high-quality data from dyadic interviews is possible only when the participants engage in conversations that meet the research purposes. At a minimum, the participants in each pair need to feel comfortable talking to each other about the research topic. Going beyond this minimal standard, the researcher should ask whether each participant will be interested in what the other has to say. When this kind of *mutual* interest is present, each participant can almost automatically align his or her thinking to what the other person is saying, making it easier to generate a relevant response and maintain a smoothly flowing exchange.

Common Ground as a Criterion

As noted in the previous chapter, the things participants share in common will facilitate their ability to understand each other and help to establish a flow of interaction (Hyden & Bulow, 2003; Moen et al., 2010). At the most basic level, recognizing common ground makes it possible to assume a shared vocabulary with regard to the topic. Discovering other similarities in experiences and outlooks will also help to facilitate the conversation. More often than not, the recruiting criteria and the basic research topic for the study will bring together participants who have more than enough common ground to conduct a coherent conversation. However, establishing common ground does not mean finding participants who agree with each other. The point is not that they share the same perspective but that they can understand and respond to each other's views.

A useful example comes from the study with first-year graduate students, in which the recruiting criteria made sure that the participants were from different departments, which created common ground and facilitated participants' ability to speak from a distinct perspective. On the one hand, each person had a similar experience of entering and adapting to a new role. On the other hand, each could expect his or her experience in a program to be somewhat different from the other person's. This combination of obvious similarity and obvious difference helps meet the recommended standard of mutual interest recommended.

These issues also lead back to the earlier description of sharing and comparing as desirable dynamics in the conversations that make up dyadic interviews. In particular, possessing common ground means that one person's reply to the other does not need to be "Oh yeah, me too." Instead, it can be something like "I hear what you're saying, but for me ..." or "It's interesting that you say that, because things are pretty different for me." In terms of sharing and comparing, the presence of common ground means that the participants will have comparable experiences or viewpoints.

One element that has been implicit in this presentation is the preference for avoiding conflict in both dyadic interviews and focus groups (Myers, 1998). Once again, however, avoiding conflict is not the same as producing agreement. Instead, the point is to allow for the kind of differences and disagreements that interest rather than divide the participants. The kind of conflict that produces antagonism is often associated with ideological or moral differences. Such fundamental divisiveness can lead the participants to stereotype each other and treat the other person as little more than a member of a disliked category. Disagreement at that level is likely to produce interaction that consists of little more than posturing around predetermined positions. Avoiding conflict thus goes back to the minimal need for these particular participants to feel comfortable talking to each other about the particular topic.

Dealing with Sensitive Topics

The extent to which a topic raises sensitive issues is an important consideration in dyadic interviews. One frequent issue when one is creating conversations about sensitive topics is whether participants will limit what they are willing to say about themselves. In particular, there is a concern that each participant will withhold potentially discrediting information rather than reveal it to the other person. In technical terms this is known as under-disclosure. The idea of under-disclosure comes from Uncertainty Reduction Theory, in which Berger and Calabrese (1975) describe disclosure in general as a tactic that people use as they get to know each other. Under-disclosure captures the idea that sharing sensitive information is less likely when two people are just getting to know each other, because each person is uncertain about how the other person will react. Over time, as the relationship develops, that shared experience clarifies which kinds of things are safe to discuss.

The most common strategy for dealing with under-disclosure is through careful attention to the participants' shared relationship with the topic. Composing pairs who are likely to share common ground with regard to the topic allows each person to make an initial set of assumptions about what the other already knows and understands. An example is the study about Asian American and Pacific Islanders who shared a history of substance abuse. Although revealing a personal history of substance abuse would definitely be a sensitive topic in many contexts, this is not the case when each person already knows that his or her partner has a similar history. For this study, the participants were not only willing to discuss their substance abuse but also equally interested in what each other had to say.

If dyadic interviews follow the same path as focus groups, over-disclosure may be as large a concern as under-disclosure. In the classic view from Uncertainty Reduction Theory, over-disclosure can be problematic for relationship development, because one participant reveals things that go beyond what the other finds comfortable. Here, however, the relationship between the participants may last no longer than the interview itself. The relative anonymity of these short-term relationships can change disclosure dynamics. This situation is especially likely to occur when one or both participants have had little opportunity to discuss a sensitive topic with others who not only understand their perspective but also have stories of their own to tell. This unusual degree of comfort around discussing a "taboo topic" can erase the usual lines around over-disclosure.

To the extent that the researcher has clearly defined boundaries about which topics are safe for the current conversation, over-disclosure means that the participants are going beyond the desired limits. If participants exceed these limits, it raises ethical issues. Thus, when dealing with sensitive issues, one should have both a clear sense of the boundaries for appropriate disclosure and a plan for how to redirect the conversation if the participants begin to go too far. One important reason for having this explicit level of preparation is that over-disclosure often moves very rapidly once it starts, because the participants often find it highly rewarding to talk with another person who understands the very things that they can seldom reveal to anyone else. The easiest way to deal with this situation is to use the initial instructions for the interview, first to establish boundaries and then to warn the participants that, if they start to move beyond those boundaries, you will slow things down and go back to the original topic. This way, you have established a basis for interrupting and redirecting the conversation if it strays into unsafe territory.

Homogeneity as a Strategy for Pair Composition

The most typical response to issues such as common ground and sensitive topics is to bring together homogeneous pairs of participants. Of course, this raises the question of "homogeneous in with regard to what?" The answer is "with regard to the topic they will be discussing." As indicated in the sections on common ground and on sharing and comparing, the easier it is for participants to establish familiarity, the higher the quality of the conversation they are likely to have. For example, in the study involving people with early cognitive impairment, the participants were not familiar with each other's life situation but were aware of their potential communication difficulties. And, in the study of substance abuse among Asian American and Pacific Islanders that brought together partners with matching cultural backgrounds and personal challenges, this dual degree of homogeneity helped to make it possible to discuss an extremely sensitive subject.

Demographic homogeneity seldom occurs. Too often, researchers want to pursue rather mechanical criteria for pair comparison, but the real issue is whether simple similarities on criteria such age, gender, ethnicity, and so on provide enough common ground to sustain a productive conversation. Thus, in the study involving people with early cognitive impairment, the participants were all older, but this fact was incidental to the relationship between aging and dementia. Alternatively, the study on first-year graduate students primarily involved young adults, but that fact was also incidental to the category of participants being studied.

Segmentation to Create Homogeneity

Segmentation sorts the dyads into subsets, each of which has its own specific composition criteria. One easy way to think of this arrangement is that the segments correspond to different categories of participants. Among the examples, the study on Asian and Pacific Islander substance abuse is the only one that involves segmentation. In that study there were two major segments, one that involved pairs of substance abusers and one that involved staff from the treatment center (in addition, there were a small number of interviews with community leaders for background purposes). These pairs were all homogeneous in the sense that substance abusers were paired only with substance abusers and staff members were paired only with other staff members.

Creating homogenous segments serves two purposes, one that benefits the participants and one that benefits the research team. For the participants, homogeneity once again assures that they are interacting with a peer who shares a similar relationship to the research topic. This arrangement is particularly useful for facilitating comfortable interactions such as sharing and comparing. For the research team, segmentation allows direct comparisons between the different categories of participants. These comparisons are particularly useful for analytic purposes, because they give the researcher a clear view of the similarities and differences between the groups. Segmentation can thus be described as a design strategy that creates both homogeneity within pairs of participants and differences between those pairs.

Possibilities for Mixed Pairs

Just because homogeneity is the most common approach to pair composition does not mean it is the only option. Instead, heterogeneous, or "mixed," dyads may be a useful option. Within the examples described here, the one on social services for elderly residents of low-income housing made the strongest use of heterogeneity. In that study the pairings brought together service providers who typically had different occupations—or, if they did have similar jobs, they came from different agencies. In addition, there is an element of heterogeneity in the study on graduate students, because each participant came from a different discipline. In both cases, the interaction went quite smoothly, and the content of the discussions was as interesting to the participants as it was to the researchers.

The reason why heterogeneity worked in both of these studies was a combination of the participants' common ground and their unique experiences with the research topic. This combination was especially useful because it provided a natural basis for sharing and comparing. On the one hand, learning that they shared similar experiences and feelings despite their differences led to conversations about what produced this similarity. On the other hand, comparative differences are to be expected, and once they are encountered they could be explored. Thus, regardless of whether participants uncovered similarities or differences, they had something to talk about. Note, however, that there still needs to be some relatively obvious element of common ground, which is typically related to the mutual relevance of the research topic. Interestingly, a shared interest in but different orientation toward the topic does not necessarily guarantee common ground at the level of a shared vocabulary. Between the two examples mentioned previously, the pairing of social service providers for the elderly generated more cultural difference in ways of relating to similar concerns, while the shared institutional basis for graduate school typically made it easy to translate experiences from one program to another.

Comparing dyadic interviews to focus groups, one notes a distinct difference in how they handle heterogeneity. For focus groups, the more complex issues involved in generating smooth interaction among several participants has led to a strong emphasis on homogeneity (for example, Morgan, 1996; Krueger & Casey, 2014). In particular, mixed groups raise more difficulties with common ground because the heterogeneity across the multiple participants dilutes the common ground shared by the group as a whole. If the solution to this dilemma is to create groups with more common ground, then that is the same as saying that the groups require more homogeneity

The limited information available so far indicates that the issue of heterogeneity may not pose as strong a limitation in dyadic interviews. When there are only two participants, it appears to be easier to negotiate a consensual basis for their conversation. Of course, this kind of pairing still requires careful consideration, both to be sure that the topic generates sufficient common ground and to avoid the kind of differences that are likely to produce conflict. Within this rather broad range of differences, it is definitely worth considering the possibilities of using mixed rather than homogeneous pairings of participants.

Special Case Concerns in Pair Composition

Along with these general guidelines, there are a number of specific circumstances that require consideration in pair composition. The following sections cover asymmetry in relationship-based dyads, previous acquaintanceship, and differences in power or status. Of course, this brief list by no means exhausts the special cases that may require attention.

Asymmetry in Relationship-Based Dyads

The issues posed by relationship-based dyads have already been described in detail, but one topic that needs further attention is asymmetry in the dyadic relationship. Asymmetry occurs when there is some basic difference between the partners, such as in parent-child dyads or couples in which one person is a caregiver for the other. In this situation, a fundamental decision must be made about conducting either homogeneous or mixed interviews. In the current literature, almost all the attention has been on dyadic interviews that are mixed with regard to the asymmetry, such as when teenagers are interviewed together with their mothers, or when caregiving spouses are interviewed jointly with their care-receiving spouse. When this is considered to be a problem, the most frequent alternative is to shift to separate interviews with each half of the original pair.

Rather than posing this situation as an issue of doing dyadic versus individual interviews, one could use a different alternative and create separate sets of dyads that share the same position with regard to the topic. For the previous examples, this approach would create pairs of mothers and pairs of teenagers, or pairs of care-giving spouses as well as pairs of care-receiving spouses—essentially the equivalent of segmentation as a strategy in pair composition, because there are separate categories of homogeneous dyads. One unique issue raised by this kind of design is whether there should be a direct correspondence between the asymmetric pairs of participants, so that the two mothers in one interview would have their children equivalently paired in one of the other dyads, and so on. If this kind of exact pairing is not necessary, then the mothers and their children could be treated as separate pools for composing dyads, which would clearly be a less restrictive design.

The advantage of working with homogeneous rather than asymmetric pairs is to assure greater privacy within the peer pairs; the disadvantage is the greater complexity of the recruitment. One way around this problem is to recruit the respective dyads to come at the same time and then have them take part in parallel interviews. Thus, there would be two mother-child dyads, but neither mother would be paired with her own child. This method has the limitation of requiring two interviewers—one for each dyad—but when that is possible this kind of "cross-mixed" design can be quite powerful.

Previous Acquaintanceship

There is a trade-off between very high levels of common ground and the need to work with the shared experiences and attitudes that are already part of ongoing relationships. One common expression for the latter issue is the need to "unpack" shared assumptions so the researcher can be an equal party to the mutual understandings that acquaintances can take for granted. When this unpacking is included in the ongoing conversation, the resulting information can be quite valuable to the interviewer. In particular, having a history in common is not the same as having identical experiences, so the goal is to find a way to work with existing similarities to accomplish both sharing and comparing. One way to do this is to tell the participants that you are particularly interested in hearing about ways that they are either similar or different and then to ask questions that make those aspects of the relationship especially relevant.

This is another instance in which the more complex issues posed by focus groups have made studies that use previous acquaintanceship relatively rare (but see Kitzinger, 1994 for an exception). The difficulty is with recruitment, because this design implies that all the participants are acquainted with each other and that they can meet at the same time and place. One example of where this can be done is with coworkers in an organization, but in general it is relatively difficult. This hurdle is not nearly so high when one is working with two people at a time. Snowball sampling, whereby the first participant helps to recruit the second one, can also be a useful strategy (note that Hoffman relied on this approach to create acquainted pairs in the example on substance abusers).

Differences in Power and/or Status

Hierarchy is a factor that can make it very hard to carry on a smooth conversation. Even when both participants share a link to the topic, there is typically a tendency for the person in the lower position to defer to the higher-status person. In addition, this kind of hierarchical difference is not limited to formal roles. In particular, one-sided expertise that indicates more knowledge about or more experience with the topic can confer a higher status. The best way to deal with this potential problem is to avoid it by setting careful criteria for participation, which could include screening participants about their level of expertise.

Differences in power can also produce ethical issues, most notably when the participants have an ongoing relationship. One obvious example would be a combination of a boss and someone who works for him or her. This kind of paring immediately raises issues about asking subordinates to share potentially private information with their supervisors. Even though ethical issues alone should be enough to avoid such pairings, they are also likely to produce poor quality data, because the potential outcomes for at least one of the participants can be quite threatening.

The Importance of Recruitment

Effective pair composition depends on the successful recruitment of the participants. If the recruitment fails, even well-chosen questions in the hands of a skilled moderator are useless. Unfortunately, the actual work of recruitment is too often treated as a secondary issue that doesn't receive sufficient attention.

The key to successful recruitment is the communication between the research team and the potential participants, beginning with an initial contact that emphasizes the importance of agreeing to participate. This emphasis should include making it clear that it is a two-person interview that can't happen if the person doesn't attend. This reinforces the point that not showing up for the interview will be a problem for both the researcher and the other intended participant. In addition, there needs to be further, consistent communication with the participants, such as sending a map when appropriate. At a minimum, further communication should include a reminder email or phone call on the day before the interview.

The most common result of a recruitment problem is that only one person shows up, and a possible response is to conduct an individual interview. In cases where recruitment is especially problematic, it may make sense to plan, right from the start, for a project that includes both individual and dyadic interviews. One crucial element in this approach is to have interview questions that work equally well for each type of interview. This preparation may well involve two sets of interview guides that cover essentially the same topics, but the format of the specific questions varies. Because of what is known about questions for individual interviews (for example, Rubin & Rubin, 2011) and for dyadic interviews (next chapter), this task should not be overly challenging. This approach does, however, require preparation, rather than the potentially faulty assumption that questions designed for a dyadic interview will work equally well in an individual interview.

Over-recruitment is another frequently used tactic for dealing with recruitment problems. With dyadic interviews, this typically means inviting three people to each session. If all three people show up, one option is to conduct a triadic interview. This approach is problematic, however, because very little is known about triadic interviews, and there are no sources of advice about how to devise sets of interview questions that would work equally well with either two or three participants. Another strategy is to accept the first two people into the interview and reschedule the third person—along with giving that person any reward or payment that was promised for participating.

Ultimately, recruitment has to be a core part of the research planning process for dyadic interviews. It cannot be treated as a mechanical or clerical task that can be handed off to someone else. Instead, it requires careful attention from the research team.

Conclusions

Because the issue of pair or group composition does not come up in individual interviews, the most relevant comparison is between dyadic interviews and focus groups. Much of the advice from the literature on focus groups is highly relevant, including issues such as building on common ground and avoiding outright conflict. One potential difference between dyadic interviews and focus groups is the effectiveness of bringing together heterogeneous or mixed pairs in dyadic interviews. At this point, however, the evidence for the ability of dyadic interviews to handle more diverse pairings is still preliminary, and further investigation of this possibility is an area for future research.

7. Writing Questions for Dyadic Interviews

Like each of the other design elements for dyadic interviews, writing questions requires balancing what is important to the research team and what is important to the participants. In this case, there needs to be equal attention to the researchers' interests in hearing as much about the topic as possible and the participants' interests in having a satisfying conversation. The goal is to create a set of questions that create a comfortable, free-flowing discussion of the research topics. Fortunately, there is a consider amount of attention to these issues in the literature on individual interviewing (for example, Spradley, 1979; Kvale & Brinkman, 2008; Rubin & Rubin, 2011) and focus groups (Krueger, 1998), much of which can be adapted to the needs of dyadic interviews.

As always, the quality of the data in a dyadic interview depends on the quality of the conversation. This means that it may be necessary to spend time creating an easy-going connection between participants in order to produce the kind of in-depth discussion that will be most valuable for the interview as a whole. One of the key choices that researchers must make in this regard concerns the degree of structure in the interviews, which is a central issue in writing interview questions.

The Need to Get Acquainted

The idea that questions should take the participants' needs into account is particularly important at the start of the interview. In dyadic interviews, this usually takes the form of a first question that lets the participants get acquainted in ways that are relevant to the conversation topic. Each participant is naturally curious about the other, if only in a self-interested way, with concerns such as: How well will I match up with this person? What is she or he going to expect of me? Consequently, asking an initial question that helps the participants get acquainted contributes to the overall quality of the conversation.

These introductions are also a first stage in locating and building on common ground. As emphasized earlier, this common ground does not require identical outlooks on the topic; instead, it helps each participant to understand where the other person is coming from, so they both can relate in appropriate ways. One way to think of this situation is as creating *rapport* between the participants. The literature on individual interviewing often speaks of creating such rapport between the interviewer and the informant, so that there is a smooth flow back and forth. For dyadic interviews, this same objective refers to creating an easy-going exchange between the participants.

Get-acquainted questions should not be lengthy or complex. Appendix A includes the guide from the interviews with first-year graduate students, in which the first question allows the participants to get acquainted. It consists of two subquestions:

- What made you interested in graduate school, in general?
- What influenced you to pick the program that you are in now?

These topics are allocated a total of five minutes, which allows each participant two or three minutes to share a bit of background.

Although using a get-acquainted question is a natural fit for dyadic interviews, it is different from the advice about how to handle introductions in focus groups, where the emphasis is on brief self-statements as the participants go around the table one at a time. The problem is that a group of several participants cannot share all their background stories within the five minutes originally assigned to this topic. Alternatively, if everyone in the group spoke for two or three minutes, that would take up a substantial portion of the total time for the interview.

Note that a get-acquainted question often precedes the first truly substantive question. This "discussion starter" question typically comes next in line, and it is allocated a considerably longer time period.

Degree of Structure

After the opening question, the degree of structure in a dyadic interview captures the extent to which the moderator exercises either more or less influence on the content and dynamics of the conversation between the participants. In more structured interviews, the balance between the researchers' interests and the participants' interests is tilted toward the moderator, whereas less structured interviews are shifted in the participants' direction. The degree of structure also involves the way in which the moderator conducts the interview, which is addressed in the next chapter. But the kinds of question that the moderator asks can be just as important, if not more so, in determining the degree of structure, because of the impact that the questions have on the nature of the interaction between the participants.

In less structured interviews, the questions are broad and open-ended in ways that let the participants discuss their own thoughts on the topic. This approach is particularly useful in projects in which the goals are exploratory and discovery-oriented. By hearing participants use their own terms to describe what matters to them, the researchers learn about the participants' perspectives. Hence, less structured interviews take a relatively hands-off stance with regard to predetermining the content of the discussion. This approach also requires giving the participants enough time to investigate different aspects of each question, which means asking fewer questions that each last somewhat longer (typically 15 to 20 minutes per question).

In contrast, more structured interviews are driven by the research team's agenda. In this case, the goal is to hear as much as possible about the specific things that interest the researchers. Rather than learning about the participants' general perspectives, the objective is to hear their in-depth and detailed responses to a carefully predetermined set of topics. Often, this involves a longer list of shorter questions (typically 5 to 10 minutes per question).

The degree of structure is a continuum rather than a pair of endpoints, and an obvious compromise would be to conduct a semistructured interview. Unfortunately, even though this terminology is widely used, it remains notoriously vague. Rather than specifying a concrete description of how to conduct interviews, it seems to indicate only that the interview has some structure but not too much. Few interviews are either completely structured or unstructured, so in some sense they are almost all semistructured. Thus, rather than relying on some vaguely structured midpoint, one should think in terms of the endpoints of the structure continuum.

A different issue arises in situations in which the researchers have some goals that are exploratory and unstructured, as well as other goals that are more specific and structured. Rather than trying to average out these two levels of structure, the interviewer should produce a kind of hybrid interview that contains both more structured and less structured questions. The classic format for this combination of high and low structure is a funnel, which is the topic of the next section.

The Funnel as a Common Interview Format

In funnel-shaped interviews, the opening questions are less structured, followed by a set of more structured questions. The broad open questions at the beginning of the interview correspond to the top of the funnel, while the more specific question represent the narrower portion of the funnel. This ordering also means that the questions move from being more participant-centered to more researcher-directed. The concept of a funnel structure is similar to the general advice—found in texts on both individual interviews (Rubin & Rubin, 2011) and focus groups (Krueger, 1998)—that interviews should move though a set of opening, transition, key, and closing questions. Taken together, that progression of questions generates a funnel shape.

Beginning the interview with less structured questions helps to meet the needs of both the participants and the researchers. In particular, using opening questions that are closer to the participants' point of view makes it easier for participants to start their discussion. It also makes sense for the researchers to hear the participants' thoughts before explicitly raising the topics that concern the researchers themselves. This step is especially useful for uncovering topics that did not occur to the research team before they heard them in the conversation. This funnel-concept of ordering thus makes it possible to engage in a certain amount of discovery before leading the participants in a more predetermined direction.

For the graduate school study, the second question (see Appendix A) occupies the top of the funnel: "What is grad school like, now that you are here?" This serves as the discussion-starter question, and it makes the early portion of the conversation less structured by asking the participants to talk about their experiences without specifying the desired subject matter. In essence, the participants are free to talk about any aspect of the overall research topic. This kind of openness promotes the opportunity to "share and compare," as the participants explore their similarities and differences with each other.

The breadth of this question is also reflected in the three probes that are suggested for the interviewer to use as tools for extending the conversation. Note that these probes are each quite general and free of any substantive content. Their purpose is to help to keep the conversation going and encourage participants to raise a broad range of topics.

We want to hear about:

1. Everything that matters—anything that makes a difference for you;
2. As many different topics as possible;
3. As much detail as you can give us, so use examples and stories;

In this interview guide, questions 3–6 make up the middle of the funnel, which shifts toward researcher-oriented topics. These four questions capture the research team's interest in the topics of:

4. Life outside school;
5. Classes, professors, and programs;
6. Emotional and personal reactions to graduate school;
7. Personal goals and expectations.

The goal is to hear about each of these topics in depth and detail, and this goal is also evident in the probes for each question, which are devoted to extending the discussion of the specific content for each question. (These probes are all optional, in the sense that they are primarily to be used if the conversation slows down or if it is limited to just one or two elements of the overall question.)

The final element of the funnel is typically a very narrow "wrap-up" question that creates closure for the conversation. In the sample guide, the seventh and final question asks each participant to offer a statement imagining his or her future after graduate school. This request for each participant to speak separately is a traditional feature of wrap-up questions in both focus groups and dyadic interviews, because it creates a distinct difference between this closing question and the earlier, interactive process.

Alternative Interview Formats

Although some version of the funnel is undoubtedly the most common format for qualitative interviewing in general and dyadic interviews in particular, there are a number of alternatives. Compared to the all-purpose utility of the funnel format, each of the three choices covered below tends to be associated with more restricted objectives.

Inverse Funnel

Interviews that move from more specific to more general topics are often referred to as inverse funnels (also known as inverted or reverse funnels). Here, the narrowest topics come first, with each successive question tapping into a broader aspect of the research question. This approach works well when the participants may not have thought very deeply about a topic, even if they are generally familiar with it. In that case, it is often difficult to launch into a discussion about the more abstract issues involved, so beginning with specifics opens up the participants' thinking with regard to the topic as a whole. The overall goal is to generate a more conceptual conversation than would have been possible without first talking more concretely.

One frequent starting point for inverse funnel interviews is with storytelling. Following a get-acquainted question, each participant gets the chance to tell a story related to the topic, followed by a request to compare stories. This request amounts to a two-part question: obtaining the initial stories is followed by asking the participants to expand on the ideas and experiences in their stories. To broaden the conversation, the next question could ask the participants to build on their stories by making a list of all the things they can think of that might be involved in the topic; then an additional question could ask them to think about the relationships among the items on their list. As with the traditional funnel, the inverse funnel almost always ends with a brief wrap-up question that creates a sense of closure.

History Taking

In contrast to the funnel format, the history-taking interview approach follows a linear, sequential path, with each question operating at essentially the same level of abstraction. This approach is similar to a medical intake interview that begins by asking about the first events that are relevant, followed by the next set of developments, and so on. History taking is especially useful for any topic that involves a series of events tied to a developmental or biographical process.

Decision making is a notable example of the experiences that can be investigated by this arrangement of questions. When both participants are facing or have already made a decision, history taking allows them to compare the paths that they followed and the factors that led them to similar or different outcomes. After the usual get-acquainted question, the next question could ask the participants to think back to when they first became aware of the issue that would be at the center of their future decision making, followed by a question about the changes that occurred as the experience unfolded, and ending with questions about the issues involved in the decision itself. Throughout, the questions should emphasize not only hearing about things in a descriptive fashion but also learning about what made a difference at each stage.

Brainstorming

The goal in brainstorming is to generate as many ideas as possible and then to work with those ideas. The most common format has each person generate a list of responses to the basic question, and then the two participants work together to combine their separate lists. Typically, this follow-up question to consolidate the lists also asks the participants to organize their joint list into a set of categories and to enlarge the overall list by both creating new categories and adding as many relevant items as possible to each category.

The tendency to produce relatively thin data has been a concern with brainstorming interviews for both individual interviews and focus groups, and this problem applies to dyadic interviews as well. If the idea is simply to generate a well-organized list of ideas, then brainstorming will fulfill that function. One option for taking this kind of questioning to the next level is to ask the participants to choose the best idea(s) in each category and explain the basis for their choices. Another option is to have the participants group the categories into a more complex form of organization such as a concept map, which is described in the following section.

Additional Options

There are several other interviewing techniques that can be especially effective in dyadic interviews. All the questioning strategies described here were originally developed for individual interviews and have been adapted for focus groups, but there are at least three reasons to believe that they may be more effective in dyadic interviews than in group discussions. First, the greater amount of time available for each person in dyadic interviews, in which two rather than several participants are involved, makes it more efficient to accomplish relatively time-consuming tasks. Second, some kinds of questions work better in a back-and-forth conversational exchange rather than in the multipart dynamics of group discussions. Finally, more complex exercises can be easier to implement when working with just a pair of people rather than with a larger group.

Start-Up Stories

The idea of using one of the beginning questions to request stories was discussed earlier as part of the inverse funnel format, but responses that take the form of personal stories often supply desirable interview data in a variety of interview formats. Beginning the interview with story-telling is also a good way to encourage more stories and examples throughout the conversation. Furthermore, starting with having the participants share stories helps with the process of getting acquainted that is typical of dyadic interviews.

This kind of question usually includes a period of time that is allocated to developing and rehearsing the stories. The main problem to avoid is having one of the participants tell stories that are notably longer or more elaborate than the other's. One useful way to deal with this situation is to give the participants a timed rehearsal period, so that each participant can think through two or three stories to share. In practical terms, this typically amounts to giving participants two minutes to think about the topics for their stories and mentally go over their stories, while the interviewer announces the elapsed time at 30-second intervals.

If both participants tell two stories that each last two or three minutes, this will total ten to fifteen minutes, including the two minutes for generating the stories. By comparison, spending this amount of time in a six-person focus group would allow each person to tell only one story. Potentially even more troubling for focus groups is the one-at-a-time presentation of these stories, which goes against the classic goal of getting the participants to interact with each other. This latter issue is less of a concern in dyadic interviews because there is time to share multiple stories, and this process of exchanging stories can be an effective way to start the conversation.

This comparison between the effects of size and group dynamics in dyadic interviews and focus groups illustrates how it can be easier to adapt questioning strategies from individual interviews to two-person interviews. In a one-to-one interview, it is often straightforward to begin with a question such as "Tell me a story about...." Similarly, a dyadic interview could begin with "I'd like you to share stories about...." This same prompt might work as a question for a focus group, but the consequences that it would produce in terms of timing and discussion format would be very different from those in a dyadic interview.

Grand-Tour Questions

The grand-tour approach has the participants walk through some process, step-by-step. A classic example is having people with similar jobs reconstruct a typical day, starting with their arrival at work. This is similar in some ways to a history-taking format, except that grand-tour questions usually concentrate on more routine activities and ways of doing things, while history taking usually deals with one significant experience. In general, grand-tour questions fit well with any topics that have the participants involved in some process—examples are "Tell me how you ..." and "How does it start, what happens first?" This start is followed by a continuing sequence of questions that ask for information about what happens next.

In a dyadic interview in which the participants have similar sorts of experiences, the goals are to ensure that their reactions to each other do not omit anything and to fill in details for the various steps in the overall tour. Alternatively, the two participants may have somewhat different experiences, so that working their way through the process will encourage sharing and comparing as they discover both similarities and differences in their ways of doing things. Either way, grand-tour questions are commonly followed by "mini-tour" questions that seek more depth and detail on specific steps within the overall process. These mini-tour questions thus elicit more depth as the participants describe their experiences with each portion of what they outlined in their grand-tour responses. (For more about both grand-tour and mini-tour questions, see Spradley, 1979.)

Compared to focus groups, dyadic interviews can offer an advantage regarding grand-tour questions, because of time issues and the increased complexity of using a group discussion format. On the one hand, starting the group by having each participant "give a tour" is just as time consuming as having participants tell stories one at a time, if not more so. On the other hand, having participants collaborate in constructing their grand tours is likely to be more complex than a one-to-one conversation, and such complexity is especially likely when each participant has a somewhat different account to give.

Concept Mapping

Creating mental maps is a specific kind of task that the participants collaborate on. The basic idea is to take a list of concepts that contribute to the topic and organize them in terms of their connections to each other. Like several of the other question formats, concept mapping operates as a two-part process, whereby the process of constructing the map is followed by an interpretation of why the map looks the way it does. (See Morgan, Fellows, & Guevara, 2008 for a discussion of how to accomplish concept mapping in focus groups.)

The first crucial element in creating a concept map is the list of items that will make up the map. In some cases, the research team provides a predetermined list of concepts, and in others the participants begin by generating their own list. Either way, the next step is to place the items in relation to each other, typically using either a large sheet of paper or a white board. The final step is to draw and label lines between the pairs of concepts that have the most important connections. Ultimately, these maps can take a number of different shapes, including hierarchical organization charts, chains of cause and effect, and diffuse networks of linkages.

In focus groups, constructing concept maps is possible but complex (Morgan, Fellows, & Guevara, 2008). One obvious issue in conducting map construction in a group is the complexity of getting the group members to work together in a coherent fashion. In contrast, the two participants in a dyadic interview typically experience little difficulty. Thus, in an example not covered earlier, pairs of mentors for undergraduate students built maps of the kinds of problems that their advisees were most likely to encounter. Each participant generated a list of three or four problems that he or she encountered frequently; then the two consolidated their lists, placed the items on a sheet of easel paper, and labeled the most important connections between the various problems. Constructing the map took 10 minutes, followed by another 10 minutes to describe and interpret the map.

Exercises and Tasks in General

Like concept mapping, there are a wide range of potential exercises and tasks that may be easier to implement in dyadic interviews than in focus groups. Once again, the dyadic interaction is likely to be both less time consuming and less complex to put into practice. Another difference is the greater ability to make a recording of the interaction that occurs during a task in a two-person conversation than in a group discussion. For many tasks the process of negotiating the various elements of the process requires a great deal of talk, which can be very difficult to track in a multiperson give-and-take. In particular, the first, more active part of an exercise such as concept mapping typically produces less in the way of usable data than does the equivalent two-person negotiation over what to do and how to do it.

A good example would be team-based exercises, when a focus group is divided in half, with each team assigned to create something, such as the draft of an advertisement or a brief presentation (see Krueger, 1998, for this and other exercises in focus groups). In this case, most of the data comes from the second or follow-up part of the exercise, when each team describes its product and the group as a whole then compares the two results. Contrast this situation with the less elaborate process in dyadic interviews, in which each participant makes and presents something, followed by a person-to-person discussion of the two products.

Conclusions

Overall, dyadic interviews can benefit greatly from the work that has already been done on creating questions for qualitative interviews at either the individual or the group level. As this chapter demonstrates, dyadic interviews can readily accommodate many of the best practices in both areas. What remains to be explored is whether dyadic interviews produce either entirely new question formats or unanticipated variations of existing formats. This is an important area for future research.

8. Moderating Dyadic Interviews

Researchers who are new to dyadic interviewing often assume that it is the moderator's job to make the interview work. The fear is that without the moderator, the participants won't talk to each other; however, this is unlikely to be an issue in dyadic interviews. If the researchers have paid sufficient attention to recruiting participants who are interested in what each other has to say, and if they have written questions that will interest the participants, that should be more than sufficient to create a good conversation. The point is that what happens in the interviews is not solely the moderator's responsibility, because the research design as a whole helps the conversation happen.

The overall goal of generating a good conversation still leaves plenty of room for different approaches to moderating, and the importance of balance between the needs of the participants and the research team is especially apparent in making decisions about how to moderate dyadic interviews. Once again, the structure dimension is highly relevant: with less structured moderating, the balance leans toward the participants' interests, and with more structured moderating, the balance leans toward the researchers' interests. Thus, there is no "one size fits all" approach to moderating; instead, the choice should meet a clearly defined set of goals.

Structure as a Dimension in Moderating

The basic continuum for styles of moderating is the same as it is writing questions, with less structured and more structured approaches as the basic options. As before, less structured moderating emphasizes learning

Essentials of Dyadic Interviewing by David L. Morgan, 71–78 © 2016 Left Coast Press, Inc. All rights reserved.

the participants' perspectives, which means that the moderator does less to direct the discussion. In contrast, more structured moderating puts an emphasis on the researchers' agenda, which leads to a more directive approach. Of course, there is always the option of a semistructured approach, which combines elements of the two alternatives or averages out the differences between them.

The goal of a less structured approach to moderating is to emphasize hearing from the participants, in their own words and on their own terms, with only minimal involvement of the moderator. Several of the examples of dyadic interviews described in a previous chapter show that it was quite easy to maintain a less structured approach to moderating because of the participants' shared interest in learning about each other. This situation was particularly apparent in the study that involved physicians talking to each other on the telephone about their experiences with computer-based record keeping. In that case, the moderator was quite pleased with the participants' ability to carry on their own conversations, which almost automatically covered all the topics on the interview guide, giving the moderator an opportunity to listen to and learn from the participants.

More structured approaches to moderating essentially reverse the priorities of less structured approaches. Here, the moderator takes a more active stance, with a notably higher level of engagement throughout the interview process. In more structured dyadic interviews the moderator can maintain a lively conversation between the participants while also retaining considerable control. The risk is that the interview will turn into a serial format, in which the participants take turns talking to the moderator and thus communicate less with each other. In general, the issue of how to conduct more structured dyadic interviews has received relatively little attention; all five of the detailed examples presented in Chapter One fall toward the less-structured end of the continuum.

Setting Up a Moderating Style

Although most people think of moderating as something that happens after the first question is asked, the process of creating a less structured or more structured moderating style starts with the first contact between the participants and the moderator. From the beginning, this is a question of impression management—the moderator is either relaxed and simply present or more formal and in charge.

This difference in moderating style is readily apparent during the preliminary introduction to and the instructions for the interview. According to the traditional steps in conducting an interview, the first thing that happens is that the interviewer explains such things as goals and ground rules. During this time, the interviewer is the center of attention, which can be a resource for creating a more structured style of moderating, because it creates a relatively easy transition from giving directions to being directive. By comparison, setting up a less structured moderating style may require a series of more explicit statements about how the group will operate.

For both less and more structured moderating, one of the key elements of the instructions is the description of the expected roles for the moderator and the participants. With less structure, this means portraying the moderator as someone who does more listening while the participants have the primary responsibility for carrying on the conversation. One useful strategy for less structured moderating is to take on the role of a note taker—someone who pays careful attention to what people are saying without getting directly involved in their conversation. Regardless of the strategy being used, the goal is to get the participants to think in terms of their own responsibility for keeping things going rather than treating the moderator as a leader.

In contrast, in more structured interviews the moderator will talk about the active role he or she will play. For instance, the idea that the interview as a whole is driven by the research team's agenda can be embodied by the questions in the interview guide. This strategy has moderators portray themselves as timekeepers who need to manage a series of questions. The overall picture is of a moderator who plays an active role while the participants may need to downplay their own interests to meet the moderator's needs.

During the Conversation

A basic principle is that the less the moderator does, the more the participants will do. When the moderator talks more, participants will assume that their job is to listen. When the moderator asks more questions, they will assume that their role is to answer the questions that are put to them. When the moderator calls on people, they will wait to be called on. And so on.

In many ways, this is an issue about who is the center of attention, moderator or participants. Moderators using a less structured style may have their heads in their notes, giving occasional nods and smiles to encourage the flow of the conversation. Moderators using a more structured style may actively use probes such as to request more information or directing when participants respond to each other—for example, "What do you think about that?" Either way, the moderator's self-described role from the introduction and instructions is now put into play in ways that reinforce the general level of structure.

In creating and maintaining the level of structure, one should match the moderating style with appropriate questions. This matching needs to happen throughout the interview, but it is especially important during the transition from the instructions stage to the interview itself. As noted, the moderator begins as an unavoidable center of attention, so the first questions either shift this role for less structured moderating or strengthen it for a more structure approach. For the get-acquainted question, a less structured approach would be to let the participants get acquainted entirely on their own, whereas a more structured approach might include a more formal process of introductions.

These same issues continue during the first real "discussion starter" question. For example, in an earlier version of the graduate student interview guide (Appendix A), instead of generally dealing with what graduate school is like, the second question gave participants the task of making a list of "all the important things that go into being a graduate student." In this case, a simple difference in how the moderator works with the ongoing list construction can reinforce a less structured or more structured approach. Both options involve the moderator keeping a list, but the difference is in how this role is explained. For less structured moderating, this would be something like "I'll keep track of the things you say, and that way you can just have a conversation, while I put together a list." Alternatively, a more structured approach might be "As you're talking, tell me the things that should go on the list, and I'll write those down for you."

Whatever the degree of structure, one important standard is that the moderator should be acknowledging each person's participation in the discussion, as opposed to responding directly to the *content* of what each person says. Thus, anything that contributes to the conversation gets rewarded by nonverbal responses, such as smiling, or semiverbals, such as "yeah" or "unh-hunh." This form of acknowledgment is quite different from anything that signals a positive or negative judgment on the substance of what participants say. In general, moderators thus preserve their neutrality with regard to what is being said while freely encouraging the participants to generate an active conversation.

Working with the Topic

An issue that comes up in any form of interview is what to do when the participants are getting off topic. The strategy for handling this depends on the goal for the research, which can easily be summarized by the structure distinction. On the one hand, the exploratory goals that are typically associated with less structured interviewing suggest a slower response to a conversation that appears to be moving away from what was anticipated. This situation allows for the possibility of hearing new ideas that didn't fit into the research team's initial expectations. On the other hand, the agenda-driven approach that typically goes with more structured interviewing will lead to a quicker reaction—which assures that the interview provides depth and detail on the desired topics without wasting too much time on things that fall outside this area. If it does become clear that the participants are getting too far off topic, then the most common tactic is to remind them of the topic with a few key words or phrases from the original question, such as "We seem to be getting a bit far from our topic of...."

Moderators also have to make a choice about what to do when participants start getting into the specifics of a later question. This situation only partly represents a matter of ordering, because there is usually a sense of how long each question should last in order to generate sufficient material on the topic, so moving on to a second topic risks cutting the first one short. The flexibility of less structured moderating once again points to letting the participants pursue their own direction. If the participants don't automatically return to the first topic at some point, then it is relatively easy to reintroduce it: "One thing you were talking about earlier that I'd like you to say more about is...." In contrast, a more structured interview guide should include information about approximately how much discussion should be devoted to each question. In this case, the moderator is more likely to interrupt with a request to stay on topic: "You're getting into something we've got on the schedule for you to talk about in a little bit, but for now, let's hear more about...."

One place where the distinction between less and more structured approaches doesn't hold up is in a classic funnel format, which blends the two. From a moderator's point of view, this involves a change in style, from the less directive role at the start of the interview to a more directive role in the center of the funnel. This switch is seldom difficult, however, because the broad, open-ended questions at the beginning have almost always raised some version of the topics that make up the rest of the research agenda. Moving from broader to more specific questions often makes it easy to pick up on what the participants have already said as a way to make the transition with a statement such as "One thing that you've already mentioned that I'd like to hear more about is...." If the participants haven't mentioned anything on a topic that was expected to be part of their conversation, the moderator can inquire: "One thing that you haven't mentioned yet and that I'm curious about is...." This approach makes it possible to turn around what participants have said so that it is interesting if they've already talked about something or equally interesting if they haven't talked about it yet.

Managing Interaction

All the researchers who worked on the examples in the first chapter had experience with focus groups, and they all reported that their dyadic interviews were easier to manage. There are several possible explanations for this. One likely reason is that two participants have considerably more opportunity to become attuned to each other, as compared to a group of people who must simultaneously pay attention to several other people. A second explanation is that in dyadic interviews there is a basic conversational dynamic whereby as one person finishes speaking, the other person is required to respond in some coherent fashion that moves the conversation along—as compared to a group discussion in which it can be uncertain who will or won't comment next. Finally, these two processes go together to produce a difference in the norms of politeness for two-person conversations, where each person creates opportunities for the other to speak.

From a moderator's point of view, the classic issue with regard to interaction is when someone is talking either less or more than desired. This concern can occur in both dyadic interviews and focus groups, but the arguments already mentioned point to fewer problems in dyadic interviews. Still, it is at least conceivable that the contributions from the two participants become so unequal that what should be a conversation is closer to a monologue—although the collective experience from the examples described earlier did not find any interviews that actually exhibited this problem.

When there is an imbalance in how much the two participants talk, the first consideration is whether it is due to personality characteristics. Some people simply talk either less or more than others as part of their normal conversational style. If so, they may well be aware of this habit, which also means that they are likely to respond to straightforward requests from the moderator. A good place to work on the dynamics of interaction between the participants is at the start of a new question. Note that it may be difficult to tell whether unequal levels of participation are due to one person having a tendency to talk more or the other person to talk less, so a strategy that works equally well in either circumstance is to say something like "I'm hearing more from [Person #1], so let's give [Person #2] a chance to go first and start the discussion on this question, so we can even things up." This type of question can also be matched to probes to the quieter person, such as "Can you tell me more about that?"

When one of the participants has a tendency to ramble, it can be effective to interrupt gently by saying something like "OK, now let's give [Person #2] a chance to talk about this." This approach is noticeably different from the case where one participant is leading the conversation because she or he is more emotionally or ideologically or otherwise committed to the topic. In that case, the quieter participant may indeed have things to say but cannot get into the conversation easily. A potential moderator response is to feed back some of what the more dominant partner is saying and use that as a basis for hearing from the other person: "I hear you saying things like [repeat key phrases]; now let's hear what [Person #2] thinks about [restate question topic]." In rare instances, it may be necessary to go beyond this and reemphasize elements of the ground rules from the introduction, such as "I understand that you have some strong feelings about this, but, remember, the main reason for having two people here is to learn what both of you have to say, so let's hear from [Person #2]."

Of course, it is always possible that the difference between the two participants is indeed due to personality differences in talkativeness, and, if so, there is no reason to persist in trying to fix it. Rather than seeing every instance of unequal participation as a problem, it is better to think about whether the inequality is part of a natural variability, where most conversations are evenly balanced but a few less so. If instead there is a consistent tendency toward different levels of participation across multiple dyads, this might indicate differences in the comfort levels for some of the participants, which would in turn lead to a reconsideration of the pair composition criteria and/or the interview questions.

Conclusions

Because dyadic interviewing is so new, there is still a great deal that can be learned about moderating. One thing that is already apparent is that less structured moderating styles can be very easy to implement. As noted at the beginning of this chapter, careful attention to pair composition and question writing often makes it possible for high-quality conversation to occur with little intervention from the moderator. For a moderator who is using a less structured approach, this possibility means that he or she may be able to spend nearly the whole interview listening to the participants, with only an occasional, minimal intervention to move the participants from topic to topic within the interview guide.

The effectiveness of dyadic interviews for more structured approaches remains less certain. In part, this uncertainty reflects a lack of experience. Since all the examples considered here used a less structured or funnel-based approach, the use of more structured approaches needs attention. The issue of how to work with participants when the moderator has to pursue a carefully predetermined agenda is thus another area for future research.

9. Analyzing Dyadic Interviews

In general, the analysis issues for dyadic interviews are similar to those for individual interviews and focus groups. For example, the same range of methods that apply to other data collection methods are equally useful for dyadic interviews, including content analysis, grounded theory, and thematic analysis (each of which will be discussed shortly). Similarly, the same software programs for assisting in qualitative data analysis can be used with dyadic interviews.

One issue that does involve both dyadic interviews and focus groups, but not individual interviews, is what can be called the units of analysis trap. The trap is getting caught up in a debate about whether the individual participants or the dyads are the appropriate unit of analysis. The problem is that the concept of a unit of analysis comes from qualitative research, and this concept has little or no relevance for studying the interactive production of qualitative data (Morgan, 1996). Instead, it makes more sense to see the individuals and the dyads as inseparable. On the one hand, the dyadic interaction would not exist without the contributions of the individual participants. On the other, what each individual says is inevitably influenced by the ongoing dyadic conversation. Thus, questions about the unit of analysis for dyadic interviews are at best misguided.

Another basic question about both dyadic interviews and focus groups is just how much attention to pay to the interaction itself. Several authors have argued that reports of focus groups rely too much on individual statements, rather than giving illustrative quotations that show longer sequences of interaction (Kitzinger, 1994; Wilkinson, 1998a, 1998b; Duggleby, 2005). As noted earlier, however, the fact that interactions are the source of the content in dyadic interviews does not mean that it is necessary to analyze the interactive dynamics of those conversations (Morgan, 2010). Nor is it necessary to search out quotations that show interaction between the participants; instead, the goal should be to find the best match to the substantive point being made.

At a broader level, there is a key distinction between analyses that concentrate on either the interaction or the substantive content of what is said. To some extent, this is a false dichotomy because *what* gets said (the content) depends on *how* things get said (the interaction), and vice versa. Even so, if focus groups are a likely template for dyadic interviews, then the vast majority of that existing work has concentrated on the subject matter of the participants' discussion. The bulk of this chapter thus emphasizes analyses of the content of the conversations in dyadic interviews; before that, however, we must consider analyses that center on interaction.

Analyzing Interaction Dynamics

The earlier chapter on interaction showed that existing literature on focus groups has raised any number of issues with regard to interaction, and there is every reason to believe that similar approaches will also be relevant for dyadic interviews. Indeed, dyadic interviews may be even more promising for analyzing interaction owing to the relative simplicity of two-person interaction, as compared to the more complex dynamics in focus groups. This fact is most apparent in the fundamental concept of turn taking, whereby each shift between speakers in a dyadic interview is by definition a return to the previous speaker. Rather than attending to several potential discussion partners, each exchange is with a single other participant.

This simplicity also makes it easier to pursue substantive processes such as the discovery and development of common ground (Hyden & Bulow, 2003; Lehoux, Poland, & Daudelin, 2006; Moen et al., 2010). Rather than trying to understand what is shared among several people, we can examine this issue directly with the two participants in a dyadic interview. In particular, if the goal is to analyze the interaction for processes related to shared common ground, this process should be clearly observable in dyadic interviews.

A similar argument applies to more abstract process such as the co-construction of meaning (Wilkinson, 1998a; Morgan, 2012). In particular, the building blocks for co-construction described earlier, such as sharing and comparing points of view on conversation topics, may well be more apparent in dyadic interviews. This probability arises from the kind of mutual attunement that is necessary to maintain a two-person conversation, where there is a notable tendency for each person to acknowledge the other's input to the ongoing dialogue. This kind of exchange is visible throughout the transcript included in Appendix B.

As is often the case, previous work on focus groups has uncovered an interesting range of issues in regard to interaction, while future work on dyadic interviews offers the potential to address those issues in new ways. Of course, these propositions about the potential benefits of analyzing interaction in dyadic interviews have yet to be proved, but this area should be fertile ground for future research.

Analyzing the Content of Dyadic Interviews

As noted, nearly all the approaches that are available for analyzing qualitative data are readily applicable to dyadic interview. This section considers four such approaches.

Summary-Based Reporting

The simplest way to analyze dyadic interviews is through a descriptive account of the primary topics in the interviews. Although this sort of analysis may not be adequate for many academic purposes, it is well suited to other goals, such as producing a final report from an applied research project. The typical goal in this approach is to determine which topics were most important to the participants. A simple standard for judging importance is whether a topic arose in nearly every interview, as well as the extent to which it engaged the participants when it did arise. For example, the graduate student interviews nearly always developed the theme of a conflict between the demands of graduate school and the ability to maintain a life outside school, and whenever one of the participants raised this topic, it was highly likely that the other person would respond in kind, resulting in an extended and lively discussion of concerns about time management and the need to balance or juggle priorities.

Note, however, that what matters is not just the frequency with which a topic is mentioned. The level of interest and significance that the participants attach to that topic is just as, if not more, important. This kind of interpretation does require a degree of judgment on the part of the analyst, but participants are usually not shy about indicating the topics they find especially meaningful.

In preparing summaries of a set of interviews, one particularly useful tool is to create a grid that systematically compares the responses to each question in each dyad. The format for this grid places the questions across the columns and the dyads down the rows, so that each cell contains a summary of how a given dyad answered the corresponding question. The easiest way to fill in the cells is to listen to the recording for a given dyad and then write the summaries question by question. A potentially more powerful technique, however, is to work down the columns rather than across the rows. In other words, start with the first column and compare what each dyad had to say in response; then move on the second question, and so on. Either of these comparisons can work well with segmented data, where the dyads are systematically divided into different subsets. In this case, the goal is to create both an overall summary of each separate segment and an overall comparison among the full set of segments.

Content Analysis

Various forms of qualitative content analysis can be applied to dyadic interviews (for example, Mayring, 2000; Vaismoradi, Turunen, & Bondas, 2013). Two common distinctions with regard to content analysis are relevant here: first, whether the analytic system is deductively or inductively derived; second, whether the analysis is driven by counting or by more qualitative approaches. With regard to deductive versus inductive versions of content analysis, the key difference is how the codebook is created. In the deductive version, the codebook originates outside the data itself and is imposed in a top-down fashion; this style of analysis is most common when there are existing theories that provide a predetermined system for examining the content of the data. In the inductive version, the researcher creates the codebook by directly examining the data itself; this style of analysis is especially appropriate when one is working with exploratory- or discovery-oriented projects. A third alternative is a hybrid approach that begins with a few coding categories that are established deductively, before an inductive reading of the data that fills in the more detailed codes. A classic application of a hybrid approach for dyadic interviewing would be to start with the topics from the interview guide as the broad categories and then elaborate the more specific codes according to the content of the participants' responses to those questions.

Once the data has been coded, content analysis offers a further choice according to whether those codes are used numerically or studied from a more qualitative perspective. The best-known versions of the quantitative approach (for instance, Krippendorff, 2012) rely on the counting of codes, where the codes represent easily recognized manifest content. For example, if the dyads were segmented by gender, then it would be possible to assess whether the conversations between men were different from those between women. In the more qualitative version, the codes would typically be treated as indicators of more subjective, latent content. In the example mentioned earlier of graduate students managing the demands of their schoolwork and the ability to have a life outside school, the segments that were coded on this dimension could be grouped together and their content interpreted to capture the nature of this experience. Once again, there is a hybrid version between these approaches (Morgan, 1993; Morgan & Zhao, 1993), which begins with counting codes to establish patterns in the data, followed by a qualitative reading of the relevant data to understand the process that produces those patterns.

Thematic Analysis

Thematic analysis is now the favored term for describing a general process of induction whereby the researcher reads and codes the data to understand what the participants have to say about the research topic. The most widely cited version of thematic analysis was developed by Braun and Clarke (2006, 2012), who proposed a six-step process: (1) immersion in the data through repeated reading of the transcripts; (2) systematic coding of the data; (3) development of preliminary themes; (4) revision of those themes; (5) selection of a final set of themes; (6) organization of the final written product around those themes. If these steps seem familiar, it is because Braun and Clarke have done more to systematize thematic analysis as it has been practiced under a variety of names, rather than to produce a truly new method.

One way to sense the central role of thematic analysis is to consider the sheer frequency with which themes are employed as the building blocks for reporting the results of qualitative research. In this format, the researcher begins the presentation of the results by announcing that there is specific number of themes and then uses a series of separate subsections to describe each theme with an accompanying set of illustrative quotations. Given the commonness of this reporting format, we have every reason to expect that it will be widely applied in the analysis of dyadic interviews.

Grounded Theory

One way to understand the unique nature of grounded theory as an analytic approach (for example, Strauss & Corbin, 1998; Charmaz, 2014) is through a comparison to the more generic process of thematic analysis described earlier. The first key difference is that grounded theory advocates alternating data collection with analysis. Instead of collecting all the data in one stage of the research and then analyzing it in a separate stage, grounded theory calls for engaging in analysis throughout the research process and using the emerging results from that analysis to guide further data collection. In dyadic interviewing, this method might mean changing the questions asked as some topics become well understood (that is, "saturated") and other unanticipated topics become increasingly relevant. Another option would be to shift either the interview sample as a whole or the composition of the dyads to do a more effective investigation of issues that become apparent during the ongoing analysis.

Another major difference is the more systematic nature of the coding process in grounded theory. An initial coding process, often known as "open coding," generates a detailed line-by-line series of codes that is intended to fracture the data into small segments. Next, selective coding reorganizes the fractured data into conceptual categories. Finally, processes such as theoretical coding or axial coding arrive at a compact summary of the most meaningful aspects of the data. Overall, it should be emphasized that the result of this coding process is intended to be a more abstract kind of theory than the typically more descriptive character of a set of themes. Given the popularity of grounded theory, we have also every reason to believe that it too will be widely applied to data based on dyadic interviews.

Conclusions

Reviewing the wide range of methods that are available for dyadic interviews reinforces the point that dyadic interviews are a *general* method for collecting qualitative data. As such, they fit well with available options that researchers have developed for analyzing other forms of qualitative data. Thus, for those who are already familiar with qualitative data analysis techniques, dyadic interviews will pose few new challenges. Alternatively, for those whose introduction to qualitative research comes via dyadic interviews, the lessons to be learned about analysis will provide a direct link to the existing work in qualitative research.

10. Conclusions

At this time, dyadic interviews are well established in relationship-based applications, especially in family studies, but they are still innovative for most applications. Fortunately, there are well-informed standards that are ready to be applied, so that it should be possible to use dyadic interviews in a more or less off-the-shelf fashion. At the same time, the newness of the method in most research areas means that there is a wide range of opportunities for the further development of dyadic interviews. There is thus a combination of an initial foundation for immediate use and a wide range of opportunities for further development; this chapter concentrates on the latter.

Additional Options and Future Directions

For present purposes, it helps to distinguish more general issues from specific topics related to research design. The first of these primarily addresses the place of dyadic interviews within social sciences methods as a whole, whereas the second looks at alternative ideas for conducting dyadic interviews.

General Issues

One set of agenda issues centers on comparisons to other methods—especially focus groups. The general position throughout this book has been that dyadic interviews are probably more similar to focus groups than they are different from them; however, the evidence for this claim is mostly intuitive. This raises an obvious question: when is it preferable to use dyadic interviews rather than focus groups? One notable trade-off is between the potential for greater depth produced by hearing from just two people versus the potential for greater breadth when hearing from more participants. Beyond that, there is the difference summarized here as two-person conversations versus multiperson group discussions, which is a major target for future research.

Another issue with regard to size is the place of triadic, or three-person, interviews within the gap between dyadic interviews and focus groups. At this point, next to nothing is known about triadic interviews, let alone whether they are more similar to dyadic interview or focus groups. As with the comparison between dyadic interviews and focus groups, this question also requires a method for making systematic comparisons between different types of interviews. Unfortunately, the process for making such comparisons is itself an issue for future research (but see Randle, Mackay, & Dudley, 2014, for one possible approach).

A different option at the more general level concerns the possibility of doing online dyadic interviews, specifically using video connections. Although the idea of conducting focus groups online has been discussed for decades, the social sciences have made little progress in developing this technique. Dyadic interviews may offer a distinct advantage in this arena owing to factors as simple as screen size. Further, just as dyadic interviews over the telephone mimic the naturally occurring version of this format, face-to-face interviews over the Internet may also provide a comfortable environment for those who are already familiar with this technology.

Design Issues

Even at this early stage, it is possible to specify what a typical set of dyadic interviews would look like. In terms of pair composition, the participants would be relatively homogeneous with regard to the topic. In terms of the questioning strategy, there would be a relatively well-specified interview guide, which would most likely follow a funnel format. And, in terms of moderating, the interviewer would be likely to use a relatively nondirective approach. So, for future directions, the goal is to consider the alternatives to these standard practices.

Pair composition may be the single area where dyadic interviews allow the most freedom for experimentation. As noted in the chapter on this topic, it seems likely that dyadic interviews can tolerate more heterogeneity than has been the case with focus groups. The issue, then, is how to explore this dimension. One possibility is to work with the kind of asymmetry found in some relationship-based interviews (for example, when one partner in a couple is a caregiver for another). This would bring together pairs who occupy role-based relationships but who are not necessarily acquainted with each other, such as a mentor and a mentee discussing their separate experiences in and preferences for this kind of relationship. Another issue with regard to pair composition is the range of different experiences or opinions that could be combined and still produce an interesting and mutually respectful conversation.

In terms of the questions asked in dyadic interviews, dyadic interviews already show a clear match with less structured approaches that rely on a relatively small number of broad questions, and it should be possible to explore even more unstructured approaches. The strength of dyadic interviews for this purpose is the extent to which the participants can get to know each other and build on both their similarities and their differences with regard to the topic. Hence, whenever the participants share an interest in a particularly meaningful topic, the moderator may need to do little more than refocus conversations that get too far off the subject. A different option for questioning is to develop exercises and stimulus materials that are especially well matched to dyadic interviews. Again, there is a contrast with focus groups, because it can be easier for two people to handle more complex tasks. Alternatively, it may be that some tasks require multiple participants to generate sufficient levels of activity. Either way, this is an area where there this is considerable room for exploration.

With regard to moderating, there is a different alternative to the examples described earlier, which relied on a nondirective style of interviewing. This raises the question of how well a more directive form of interviewing would work in dyadic interviews. The danger here is that the conversation could degenerate into a series of short replies, whereby the participants merely take turns responding to the moderator without engaging with each other. This can be workable in the group discussion that defines a focus group, because the participants can take turns making contributions and may find a topic of mutual interest during these exchanges. Whether it is possible to create similar opportunities in dyadic interviews remains to be seen.

Last Thoughts

It would be an overstatement to say that dyadic interviews have no past, especially given the previous use of relationship-based interviews in family studies. Still, the history of dyadic interviews as a more general method is very much in the present moment, with only a slim basis in existing work. With any luck, this book will mark a shift in interest that creates a new future for dyadic interviewing—one in which they are widely accepted as a useful addition to qualitative research.

Appendix A.
Interview Guide for First-Year Graduate Students

Introductions: First name and the department or program you are in.

1. **(Get acquainted): Give a quick picture in terms of BOTH:**
   What made you interested in graduate school in general?
   What influenced you to pick the program that you are in now?

2. **Since you've started school, what has changed in your life?**
   General probes:
   Who has an example or story?
   Think about any other changes that make a difference for YOU.

3. **How has your life outside school changed?**
   Probes if not mentioned, or very little discussion, and time allows:
   How easy or difficult is it for you manage your life inside and outside school?
   What do you make time for, and what can't you find time for?

4. **What about things at school—what has that been like?**
   Probes if not mentioned, or very little discussion, and time allows:
   Let's hear more about things that are [working well].
   Let's hear more about things that are [not working so well].
   How do you think your experiences compare to those of other students in your program?

5. **What have your personal reactions and feelings about school been like?**
   Probes if not mentioned, or very little discussion, and time allows:
   Let's hear more about your [positive] reactions and feelings about grad school.

Let's hear more about your [not so positive] reactions and feelings about grad school.

How is any of this related to your "sense of identity"?

6. **How well have things matched your personal goals and expectations?**
Probes if not mentioned, or very little discussion, and time allows:

Let's hear more about things that [have] matched goals and expectations.

Let's hear more about things that [haven't really] matched goals and expectations.

How well does your program match your goals for after school?

7. **Imagine a positive future in five years; what would you be doing?**
One person at a time:

[If there is any time left, let them discuss the things they just said.]

Appendix B.
Sample Interview from First-Year Graduate Students

MOD: Just to start with, we ask you to introduce yourselves, your first names, what department you're in, program, something like that for the get acquainted part and that will also help us capture that on the recording so when we go to type it up, we'll know which of you is which, which should be pretty obvious in this case, but we'll get you in the right programs anyway.

#1: I'm #1, and I'm in the AA program.

#2: I'm #2; I'm in the BB program.

MOD: So what I usually like to do is go back a little bit in terms of getting acquainted with what it was that interested you in grad school in general and then what led you to pick the programs you're in, and just all we're really going to do is have a conversation back and forth between the two of you, and I'm not going to do much more than listen in. We've chosen questions that should be pretty easy to talk about. What made you think about going to grad school, what made you think about picking this program, and hopefully that will be a way to start the get acquainted process, so go ahead.

#1: Why did you choose to go to grad school?

#2: I guess in my field of AA, it's pretty much not a requirement, but it's pretty standard to get a graduate degree, and so I kind of felt some pressure like I needed to go back to school and had it on the agenda in my head. Then I actually met someone from the department who teaches in the department who just really started encouraging me to apply, and I had a good connection with my job that they would help me pay for school, so it kind of seemed like I guess I have to go back, I have someone who is excited about it, and I've got work willing to go for it, so that sort of, I wanted to balance it with work. [University] was a logical option here in [city], but what about you?

#1:   I studied [other fields], and those areas of study give you a good foundational understanding about how the world works around you, but it's not a narrow enough education to make it of real value in terms of finding a job. You can make of it what you want, but I kind of felt like with those degrees, at least in comparison to something like a science degree where you're well equipped with a bachelor's, I needed to go on and get another degree. So I thought about going to law school. There were some things about that that I didn't like, so I chose the conflict resolution program because it sort of gave me the opportunity to pursue some of the things that I thought were appealing about being an attorney, which is helping people solve problems, although some lawyers create more than they solve. So I like working with people, and I like interacting with people and helping with problem solving, so conflict resolution was kind of I guess I felt could suit my needs well.

MOD: Just out of the options you guys had, how did you end up here?

R: For me it was that work/school balance, and since I was already in the city working, it just seemed like the most logical school within the city to go to, and it would be easy to do part time 'cause it's very central, then having that faculty connection was important for me.

#1:   Yeah, it was the same for me, you know, working downtown, living right across the river. My wife and I had just purchased a house when I knew I wanted to go back to school, so I wasn't very mobile to pursue other programs, so this, being in the heart of the city, made the university really appealing.

MOD: Let's shift and think about what about now that you're here, tell us about what it's like, anything that matters to you, and how it stacks up against maybe what you were thinking before you came in. Tell us about what it's like, particularly, I guess, one of the reasons we work with second-year students is you guys have had some time to really settle in, look at it for a while, where if we were just catching people in their first year, you guys hopefully have some good impressions.

#2:   I am kind of a first-year student.

#1:   Yeah, we're both at the end of the first year.

MOD: What am I saying? You're right. That's why we ask you that, no, no, yeah, I wondered why you were looking at me. I told you it's been a while since I did this.

#1:   That's all right.

MOD: Go ahead, because actually that was the thought, now you've had about a year or more, and now so you were starting, and hey, there are all those ideas you were just talking about, now let's hear what it's like. Thanks for straightening me out.

#2:   For me I guess it's been a little bit, I was expecting to take more night classes. I thought that it might work better with my work schedule, which hasn't come to be so true. I think I just had this idea in my head, not really knowing a ton about the department before I came in, that there were some people like us that are working full time and that are taking classes, and that schedules might be easier to accommodate. My work is super flexible so it ends up working out, but that ended up being kind of a significant difference for me. Overall, I've been really just really happy with the program and excited about how much I've been learning. I kind of thought it was going to be more of a side thing, or more of not necessarily the center of my life or the most significant thing, but my classes have just been really awesome, super relevant to the stuff I'm interested in. I've really been enjoying it a lot and being able to apply it to my work a lot, which I enjoy.

#1:   I think everything so far has met my expectations. I know a lot of people that go to the university like us that are working people, so they need the accommodation, and the AA program is pretty accommodating. I've been looking to take two classes a term and thought about taking three, and the option has always been there for me in terms of finding something, finding enough credits that I can take either at night or on the weekends. Like right now I'm taking a class where I go every Monday night, and then I also have a class where every other weekend we go Friday night and all day Saturday. So that works out well. Overall, the school has met my expectations and I feel like all the resources I need are here. There are some particular things about the program that are a little bit frustrating, but other than that, things are going well.

MOD: Anything that makes a difference to you in terms of what the year has been like and how well it's going?

#1:   For me just the simple fact that all of our core classes in our program are offered once during the day, one session during the day and one session at night. That's really important for me so that I can get all my core classes without having to take time off work. I guess one thing that has been a little bit bothersome is the library

95

hours. On the weekends, the library, on Saturday I think it opens at 10, on Sunday I think it opens at noon.

#2: Like on an undergrad schedule.

#1: Exactly, as if I was binge drinking on Saturday night so I couldn't get up before noon to get to the library, not that I don't still do my fair share of drinking, it's just that being so busy during the week, I need to get up super early on a Saturday or Sunday, and I'd like to go to the library, but oh well. I make it work.

#2: That's funny, I never go to the library actually. I guess that's part of why my experience feels different from a lot of people's just in that I don't feel like a student at all. I only take one or two classes a quarter, and I am trying a lot harder this quarter to make more connections to other students and to get involved with a graduate student association in my department and that kind of thing, but I have so many resources at work that I just search all the databases that I need for literature and stuff and do so much from there, but that's really funny about the library.

#1: The online resources do help, because everything is pretty much there for you, unless I need hard copies of something or just a quiet space to do work, then I can do it over the Internet.

#2: That's great about your department having all the core classes offered in the day and at night. I don't think there are that many part time students in my department. I think most people come in and get research assistantships or teaching assistantships and are going through the program very solidly and it's their focal point, so there are very few classes in the evenings. Maybe someday I'll get one of those and I can bump up my workload a little higher.

MOD: One of the things we're always interested in is any examples or stories, so you both have said it works for you or fits, something, anything that would kind of, again, tell each other what it's like. Don't tell me, the recorder will capture all of that. I'm getting some ideas here, but go ahead.

#1: In terms of?

MOD: Stories, examples, something like you say it works for me, we'd like to hear how that works, or anything you can think of through the year that's been an example where you felt like your expectations were getting met or something was going to way you wanted, like that.

#2:   For me, the class I'm taking this quarter, there's tremendous flexibility even though the scheduling stuff is always in the daytime, that's always been an issue. The class I'm taking has probably only met three times, and people are super flexible in office hours. I'm actually going to be part of the response to the Gulf oil spill at the end of the quarter, like the beginning of June, and they're being super flexible about me not being able to be here for the final exam period, when we're going to have presentations, different things, so even though I feel like I haven't had an evening class, I'm sure they're really nice. I've had professors and just personal relationships that have made it really easy for me and have made it a really good fit that people are understanding of the fact that I have other obligations and stuff. That's been awesome for me.

#1:   Sure. I think one of the things that makes it most convenient for me, like I said, the evening and weekend thing, but like I live just right across the river, right across from MLK by the Nike store, and so I take the bus to work. I work for the county so I get a free bus pass, so I take the bus to work, the gym is right up the street from work so I work out on my lunch break, and then I come to campus after work and then take the bus back home. So my life revolves around that, basically that cycle, so that I guess for me, if I was having to spend commuting time or one of those pieces didn't fit and I was having to spend a great deal of time trying to accommodate it, I think my life would be a lot more stressful. It's already a lot to handle, but the fact that it all kind of fits together nicely makes it really manageable.

#2:   That's an awesome point about transportation 'cause I forgot about that part, but my work being right on the green line, and then them just extending the green line down here, I can just hop on and be here in 15 minutes. It's quicker than any other way I could have probably gotten here, so that's been a huge part of really streamlining the whole thing, and that really just opened up as I was starting last fall, so I feel like a little green line poster or something, this is the most amazing, efficient line.

#1:   That's good.

MOD: You guys are getting into our next topic anyway, so let's go with that, and this is basically anything about how your life outside of school goes together with what you've got going on here. You both have already mentioned some things like that, but let's just broaden it out and hear about the whole picture about life inside school and how does that fit and how well does that fit with the other stuff that's going on.

#1:   It sounds like it fits your whole life, like it really revolves around school and work and all that, but it all fits together real well.

#2:   Yeah, it does. Luckily those two pieces are really connected. I would say my personal life is a little on the outside 'cause it's not, it's becoming a little harder to meet personal and mental needs with work and school driving the boat, but I think that's probably true for most grad students.

#1:   Your work and your education are very closely linked.

#2:   Does that work out for you as well, or is there more of a disconnect?

#1:   Well, truthfully working in the [government] office, if you look at it through the lens of [AA as a field], the [government] office is sort of counter to what AA advocates would propose for solving social issues, so I mean...

#2:   Kind of a last resort or something.

#1:   Right. I see the side of it that maybe a lot, so a lot of AA students, you know, they're pretty critical of the [government] system, and I'm also really critical of the justice system in general in some regard, but I also see the other side of it that there are some pretty bad people out there, people kill people, people rape people, they physically and sexually abuse children, and I don't know if, I know conflict resolution theorists have some ideas about how we could deal with those people, but realistically some of those people need to get locked up or otherwise they're going to hurt other people, more people. You've got to stop that somewhere, so working at the [government] office has kind of made me more I guess understanding of the role that the [government] plays in some of those issues, but I do look at it with a critical eye because of the AA stuff and just my world view, but I don't, like in terms of practicing conflict resolution, I don't get to integrate the practices that I'm learning at work. I don't really get to bridge that gap, which I would like to, you know. It sounds maybe for you working at [different government office] and learning the BB, there is more of a link between professionally what you're doing and educationally than there is for me in my work.

#2:   Yeah, that sounds like working in the [government] office gives you good perspective you can then bring to AA classes, because when you get so far into theory and so far into some stuff, sometimes it's good to have that real world.

#1:   Yeah, I think there's something to say for that, and, you know, there's definitely like varying degrees, like for example the [government workers], a lot of the younger ones are very conservative, fresh out of school, gung ho about fighting justice and crime, and they think you know, a lot of them think that drug use, drug possession, whatever, punish those people, but as they get older and they start dealing with more serious crimes and seeing more real world examples of what's happening as far as criminality goes, the more they mature along their path as district attorneys, the less they care about some of that. I guess the measly stuff like smoking pot or things like that, they're more concerned with people who are committing serious crimes, so it's kind of interesting to see them transition from being young and gung ho to kind of realistic about how the world actually is and what's important and the things that aren't important in the justice system.

MOD: There's work and transportation, there's probably other stuff, and again it doesn't have to get too personal, but how about all the stuff that comes from balancing all those things for school, the rest of it?

#2:   I think what you were mentioning, like fitting the gym into your cycle of how you get from one place to another, that's a big part for me too is putting running, or yoga, or something somewhere in the how I get from this place to another, or like I'll run to a yoga class, or I'll run to school if I know I don't need to bring something with me, or do different things so I can work my physical health into my life, because otherwise I'm sitting in my cubicle, sitting in class, then sitting on the bus, and then going crazy.

#1:   No outlet, yeah, for working it out. I mean, that's important for me too. I think another, obviously the financial aspect of school is probably a significant, you said that your employers help compensate you. I'm taking out loans for my tuition, or some of my tuition, taking out loans for my living expenses because that's one of the reasons I'm working is so I can cover mortgage payment, and food, and all that, but still, taking out loans for school, it's kind of intimidating because I've got $15,000 in loans from undergrad, then if you add another $15,000 for the loans for graduate school, then you've got $30,000 in loans. It's important to me to continue working so I don't have to accumulate more loans to make the long-term financial burden less onerous. What does [your employer] cover? I know that's kind of a personal question, but...

#2: No, and I work for a contracting company for [employer], so the contracting company has really great school benefits, which is awesome, so they'll pay up to $5,000 a year in tuition, but I blow through it really quick, so I'm kind of slowing my pace to one class a quarter and not taking a class this summer to make sure I don't overspend my, 'cause I have kind of a limited amount, so the finances do drive it a little bit. Luckily I'm not having to take out more loans, and I'm trying to pay off my undergrad ones too, but yeah, for me it really feels like time is the most limiting resource, and I'm just trying to figure out how much I can put there, here.

#1: So them covering $5,000 a year, does that mean that you're less concerned with how quickly you complete the program?

#2: A little bit, yeah, if I, yeah, I'd probably have a different approach if I was paying for it out of pocket. I might either try to just get through it all at once or I'd maybe not be working so much, or going maybe even less because I may not want to pay that much out of pocket myself, but it definitely impacts that way that I am going about it. It is slowing me down a little, but I also want to get through it, because I don't want to be balancing both of these things forever, 'cause it feels really like a lot.

#1: How many credits is your program?

#2: Like 45.

#1: Okay.

#2: What's the AA program?

#1: Ours is 63, which is, I kind of feel like there's a little frustration on my end because first of all 63 credits means that you go basically, like for me I'm taking eight credits, that means I have to go eight quarters of eight credits, that would be 64, so that's like two years including a summer term. That's pretty long, and then also there's a requirement for 300 hours of practicum and either a thesis or a project.

#2:   I didn't know you guys did theses projects.

#1:   So then on top of that there's just not much direction from the program about, okay, so you're a first-year student, here is your first class, where is what you need to do to get your piece of paper that says you have your CR degree, you know, not that I just want the piece of paper, I'm there for the skills, but at the same time I wish there was this real-world need to start and finish a program, because you can't just be a AA student forever.

#2:   I hear a lot of that within the BB department too, I think there's a lack of a clear-cut way to go about this, just lining up with what the steps are and how to get from point A to point B, and I also keep hearing people who have been working on their Master's for like four years, or people in the Ph.D. program that have been there for like eight, and I'm like wow, how do you just keep on doing that? And I'm very conscious about not wanting to do that, which it sounds like maybe you are too, but I don't want to, five years down the road, be like, hm, I seem to have missed something. I need to go do that.

#1:   Right, oh well, the thing about 63 credits is I have heard there are some Ph.D. programs that are about 90 credits total, so your total 90 credits of undergraduate work, so requiring 63 is almost ⅔ toward that sort of requirement, which yours is about half, which seems like it would be about right, two years for a Master's, a couple more years for Ph.D.

#2:   I think ours is a little small compared to some of the other programs, 'cause I think I looked at planning a little bit, I looked to geography a little bit when I was thinking about coming back, and I think ours is a little bit smaller than some of the others, but yeah, it's kind of nice.

#1:   That's great.

#2:   I can see how 63 would be hard to get through.

MOD: You guys are getting into our next topic again. You're making me look good, so it really is getting into what life is like inside of school, and you know, that's got a whole lot of pieces to it, so think about as much stuff as you can about now that you've been in this year, and now you're a graduate student and all of that, you know, what's that been like and what does it mean, and what do you have to do to make it work in terms of the class and the being a graduate student side instead of the balancing side and life. Now let's pick on school.

#1: For me, I don't feel like it's that bad. Let's contrast it with undergrad. In undergrad you, there's a lot of work, reading, you have to do some papers and some exams, but you can get away with a lot more, I guess just flying by the seat of your pants.

#2: Just showing up.

#1: Just showing up, handing in words on a page, and there's a little bit more where you can get away with that sort of stuff, but I guess graduate school, I'm a little more mature now, and I feel like there's nothing expected of me that shouldn't be. We don't have much, we don't have exams in my programs really, we just have papers, which I think suits the program better than exams, but I feel like it's what I expect each quarter. For each class I usually have like two papers, one 5-page paper, one 8-to-10 page paper, or one project and presentation, and a 10-page paper, so I feel like it's sort of what I expected of it, then obviously I put more time and effort into writing a more coherent paper than I did in undergrad just because in graduate school I think, I'm in graduate school because I want to learn in the subject matter, and I want to make the most of it, so if I hand in a shitty paper, then I'm only doing myself a disservice because I'm not maximizing my opportunity to learn.

#2: Yeah, I do think the quality of work is different, and I can't tell for myself whether that's all about being older and being, having a professional life and some of that stuff, or whether it's too being able to concentrate on only taking one or two classes at a time. For me, I don't think I'd want to go back to being a full time student like I was in undergrad, because there is this, I have this feeling with my Master's right now of like you could put your whole life into it, you could stay up until 5 a.m. every night researching stuff and reading more things and getting so much information and doing all that, and I think that in undergrad I felt really pressured to do that in four different subjects at a time, and I think with my Master's I'm feeling a little bit less, I don't know, I'm just making that and drawing that line more easily and more comfortably about how easily I am going to put in, and I found good systems, I think, about how to go about the quarter actually is one other thing about this whole [university] master's thing that is very different for me.

#1: Did you do semesters or something?

#2: Yeah, I was on the semester system before, and I really, really prefer it.

#1: Really, to the quarters?

#2: Yes, you just have so much more time to familiarize yourself with the subject, get into the groove of how things are going to be with the professor, requirements of the class, background, that kind of thing, and then if you have a project, if you have a paper, whatever it is, just more time to dive into it, just a few more weeks' time, but still, I think the semesters, I went to [other undergraduate school] here in [city], and I think the semesters are like 15 weeks or something.

#1: Yeah, they're longer. Was there a J term there in January or no?

#2: You had a month off between mid-summer to mid-January.

#1: And then you started the second semester when you came back?

#2: Yeah, you started second semester when you came back. I don't know, the quarter system has been a little bit for me to catch up with and figure out how to deal with, just 'cause it goes so fast and a lot of my classes do have projects, or you know, you're working with community parents, you're developing these relationships that, especially having my professional life so closely aligned, I really always want these things to go really well. Like you were saying with the paper, you don't want to turn in crap. It's like why am I paying for this? Why am I doing this whole thing? So really wanting to do quality work in a 10-week time frame I'm finding challenging, but I think the thing that I found is front loading it as much as I can and doing, really pouring a lot of energy into it on the first half of the Quarter, even if I don't necessarily know exactly what direction it might go or exactly what might happen, but I hate that end of quarter freak out thing.

#1: Yeah.

#2: I avoid it at all, I will not flip out. At the end of the quarter, I just hate that stress, but I feel like I feel more pressure in the quarter system at the end to be like crap.

#1: That does happen. I guess I've just gotten used to that, but I do freak out. I'm pretty stressed right now with everything, but it comes. I kind of like the quarter system because it goes by so quickly, so it's like you start, then next thing you know it's week six and seven, then you know, things are gearing up, you've got to get your act together, then it all goes away and it starts again.

#2:   It's over in like a week.

#1:   I know. There's something to say for that. I've never experienced the semester system, so I have no frame of reference in that regard, but I kind of like the quarters because they just go by so quick. This year, I feel like this year has just flown by. I think that's partly why.

#2:   I definitely think that's why for me too. I haven't felt time moving this fast in I don't know how long, but I think it's largely because starting the Master's program, and 10 weeks is like week one, week two, just counting down and you just keep going. It's really fast paced.

#1:   Yeah, it seems like there's just a couple of weeks between the end of September and Christmas, and then not much time between Christmas and spring break, then we're at the end of the school year. It just goes by really quickly.

MOD: What about, I've got a whole list of things here, but your department and your program, and all the kinds of pieces that go with relating to that and getting yourself together on that? Where does that fit into it?

#2:   You mean like the people or the requirements?

MOD: There's a piece on obviously professors and all that, then there's a piece on what are the requirements and the time tracks, or what to take to get where when.

#2:   The professors piece, the faculty at my department I really, really enjoyed working with, and the thing I realized, especially just recently is that they're all as insanely busy as I am, if not more so. They're all just balancing so many things, and coordinating conferences, writing this paper, flying to Japan to talk to people about this, this, and that, and I guess knowing and seeing that they're practicing and teaching and doing research I think has been really inspiring and also really educational for me, which has been cool.

#1:   Yeah, I guess for me I haven't done much networking with my professors outside of the class, and I know that's partly my fault. I know that a lot of them are available to learn more about what they're doing outside of class, and obviously they share some in class, but that would require investment on my part for meeting with them outside of class hours, which is really hard for me, especially because most of the times that are available to me are during my work hours and it's my work is not very flexible, so I kind of just go to class, do my work, and then I go home. I haven't done much networking. I have the desire to do more, I just haven't really made the opportunity to do it. At the same time, I've heard from some of my classmates that there's the perception that they're available, but like they're not really that available. So I don't know, but it works out for me just showing up in class, doing my thing, then leaving, but I think I'm probably not maximizing my opportunity to network as much as I could be.

#2:   It's true though I think with a lot of professors with the office hours being like a lot of times the periods when they get a lot of their work done, or return a lot of their phone calls, or do a lot of their things, and I had that feeling of, there was a few I've met with of I'm going to want to go into their office hours knowing exactly what I'm hoping to get out of what I'm going.

#1:   Not like what are you doing here, what do you want from me?

#2:   Yeah, whereas in undergrad or something I'd go into my professors offices and just talk, you know, explore some things, fly some ideas, see what stuck, that kind of thing, and I feel, I think as a grad student too here is a lot of expectation that you have your schedule and your plan and stuff, but I guess because everyone seems so busy, it's hard.

MOD: What about all those department expectations and the way the program is set up?

#2:   I don't understand my program that well, I have to admit. I think it's largely because I don't identify as a student primarily, I'm not that on campus, I missed orientation because of a work obligation, a couple of the chances I think when you really get yourself figured out, I think I missed some of those, but then I also just think there is some confusion, but I have a really nice and detail oriented advisor, so he's pretty with the requirements and stuff. He gets that stuff on my radar, and otherwise I just keep going.

#1:   I kind of feel there's not that much direction, like I saw saying, I don't feel there is that much direction in my program, I mean I understand that this is graduate level work and part of moving on to that sort of level of education I think requires that more effort be placed on the students to find their own direction, make what you want of this program, make your niche in the world, tie this program to the things you want to be doing in the real world, so I think some of the lack of rigidity is to help students find their own way in what they're going to do in the world, but at the same time, maybe this is just my socialization to the American education system, but I need a little bit more structure to help me figure out where it is I need to go, or what is it I need to get done with this program, what are the professional opportunities that I can have after I get this degree? I guess I don't really feel that there is much emphasis in my program about sending [AA graduates] into the professional world, like we need to equip these people so we can send them out and they can go apply for jobs and say hi, I'm a person who is well versed in interpersonal communication, interpersonal conflict, group conflict, and I can help you in your business or your whatever to solve these problems, or I can solve community conflict, or help with public policy in this way. There's a lot of theoretical talk, but not much here's how we're going to as a group go into the working world and apply these skills that we're learning. I feel like in science, or even computers, for example my wife is a medical technologist, she works in a laboratory. She went to [other university in town] and got a very specific degree, and she literally can go to any hospital in town, and she's like I'm a med tech, and they pay her really good money to do a very specific job. I have a girl friend of mine who is a computer developer. She develops basically web-based programs, and she has very specific things she knows how to do, and she can go to lots of businesses and say I'm a web developer, and they can say great, we've got some work for you, but with my degree it's like oh great, so you have a degree in conflict resolution, so nice to talk to you. There's not the same, the program doesn't have the same focus on helping us to develop skills and then learn how to present those skills in the real world so that they're valuable to people in the working world, because ultimately we all have to get jobs, we have to work, so help me get there I guess.

#2:   Yeah, I think my department is kind of similar to that because [subfield in BB], which is more the side I'm in than [different subfield in BB], is similarly about communication and about problem-solving skills, about these skills that we're developing that are not only applicable to this one tiny field or they're only applicable to this one discipline, and it's super interdisciplinary and so that not being specialized in one way I think is difficult when it comes to the job placement stuff and when it comes to how you articulate what your skills are and what your education gave you and that kind of thing. That part is difficult.

MOD: One thing I heard go by, there was some interaction with other students, and I wonder where that fits into the picture, 'cause it's another thing that can be a little different than undergrad.

#1: I enjoy interacting with my follow AA students. Everybody is kind of on the same page in terms of lots of people late 20s, they have jobs and school, school is half of their life, then family life, professional life are the other half, but then there are some people that are just AA students and they don't work, they may be TAs or some other things, but I like the people in my program.

#2: I have not had as much, I've been very concertedly trying to get to know more people in my program because I feel pretty disconnected from it. And there are people that are more into the science and people that are more into the management side, so it's like two groups within it, which is cool, I like talking to people that are more on the science side, because that's what my undergrad was in, I'm very interested still in the hard science stuff. One thing I found to be a major difference between undergrad and grad with students has been group work in Master's level classes has been amazing and wonderful, working on projects as a team and sharing workload among different people. I hated group work in undergrad. I was always having to pull the load and being like where is this thing you said you were going to do and all this stuff, and I've just been so impressed and thankful for the students I have worked with in classes because they have just been really hard working, really smart, really on it, people, and for me I think a lot of that, and maybe part of how my perception has changed on it is just that a lot of them are full-time student, so they are very committed and very dedicated all the time to school, and so I think with me having work going on, I've been able to take a step back from some of the situations, which has been nice.

#1: That's cool. Yeah, the group work thing is definitely a different dynamic than undergrad. Everyone, at least in my experience thus far has been pulling their own weight, and I have been learning a lot from the people I have been doing group work with, so that's cool. That's definitely a change.

MOD: Okay, now we're going to make a little different question here because we're getting toward the end, and this one is kind of about more the personal feelings, self-learning, emotional aspects of it, but one of the things we want to do and you guys did great there too talking about other students and where they're at is we kind of want to get a broader picture of that. Parts of it doesn't have to be so personal, but for all these different students, it's one of these things where tell us a story about someone else, and it's really supposed to be you, no, it's not like that, anything about what the personal/emotional aspects have been like for you, but also what do you think it's like for other people in the program just in general to get into grad school in your program, so anything about that kind of personal/emotional stuff?

#1: I've learned, I feel like I've been learning a lot about myself over the past year. A lot of that is sort of the area of study I'm in deals with a lot of introspective issues, you know, figuring out more about how you see the world around you and all of that, so I guess I feel like emotionally there has been a lot of growing up for me over the last year just in terms of being a little more mature, but that's kind of different from the emotional impact that school has on me. I feel like I kind of take it easy the first couple weeks of the term, then I always freak out and get all stressed and I'm a total asshole to my wife and everybody else because I'm all stressed out, but I complain about it and it's all over. So emotionally I feel like I've learned a lot in just trying to observe the way I behave and all of that, but I don't feel like it's been exceptionally, emotionally burdensome or anything, school.

#2: Yeah, it's funny because I was saying I hate doing that waiting till the very end thing, but I think that in my front loading it and going year round with school, I'm kind of just always a little more serious about things, or just a little more, I don't like being a total asshole like maybe I would be if I were super stressed at the last moment, but being more, like I always have an agenda, I always have a schedule, I always have my time and how I'm going to use it, and I think that does affect me emotionally and then also my relationships because I don't just sit around and shoot the shit nearly as much as I used to. We do nightly dinners at my house and I only make it there for some of them, and I only take those changes to sit around with a glass of wine and hang out, but I don't take as many of them as I probably should or as would keep me as personally connected to all the people in my life and probably keep me saner and more relaxed in the long term. That parts difficult, but overall I actually find school and working on my Master's a really affirming experience, like it feels good to be doing well in it and feel good about what I'm getting out of it. That part is nice and it helps make up for some of the sleep deprivation and some of the other part.

#1:   I agree with you. It's very affirming, especially if you apply yourself and do well, it's like I can do this. It's good. How much longer do you think we've got? I've got to get back to work.

MOD: Yeah, less than 10 minutes, is that going to work?

#1:   Yeah.

MOD: The next one is something you guys have covered a little bit before, that always makes it easier, but now looking at your personal goals and future expectations, you talked about what you were expecting when you came in, but you've already talked about where you want to go, then the question is how well is the program fitting for you that way, and what's that part of it like?

#2:   It's fitting in really well for me, especially since I already have the work thing going on. Yeah, I think this will help me get where I'm going. I don't have a specific career goal or a sense of whether I continue on to a Ph.D. or anything like that, but I definitely feel like the work I'm doing through my Master's is making me better at my job and is preparing me for lots of great opportunities in the future, but I don't have a specific goal or exact job title I'm trying to throw on my business card or anything.

#1:   It's kind of the same for me. I feel like I'm getting a good skill set that I'll want to apply at some point, so I feel like I'm becoming well equipped to go into the professional world, it's just a matter of figuring out exactly how I want to apply those skills and like you said, what you want to put on a business card at some point. So I don't know, I feel like I'm getting set up well professionally, but I don't know where that's going to take me exactly.

MOD: Let's ask about that. Suppose it's five years from now and we bring you back, and things have been going just the way you wanted them to, so we're going to end up on this positive note, and tell me how grad school worked out in terms of getting you where you wanted and what part it played in that successful life you have five years from now.

#2: I think a big part of it for me will be all the connections I've made with professors, and researchers, and community partners in [city] and in other parts of [state] that are all doing work that relates to my research interests and to the work I do now. I think it's helping add some credibility and some extra avenues that I get to work in at school in addition to my job, so five years from now if I'm still in the same job and if I'm still working on [city] like this, I think I would look back on the Master's program as something that really helped situate me and better understand the social landscape and just kind of really understand all the different players that are active in natural resource management issues in [state].

#1: That's a good point about the social networking stuff, 'cause I have similar hopes that the relationships I'm building now will be the relationships that help me get into jobs down the road and learning more about the field and hopefully developing relationships that will help me in the future, and I hope that some of those relationships, they'll see me and be like hey, that person is a good worker. That person is smart, they're capable, we could use that sort of person in what we're doing. So I hope it's not just like networking for my gain, but I hope I can bring something to what they're doing because that's it, there's some personal satisfaction in feeling that you're contributing a big part in what other people's needs are.

MOD: Anything else about what graduate school might do for you in terms of a positive outcome?

#1: I think ultimately a bachelor's degree seems to be the equivalent to what a high school education was maybe 30 years ago, so realistically I feel like it takes a graduate degree any more to be taken seriously. Bachelor's degree is not what it used to be perceived as in terms of someone who is a little more specialized and a little bit more well equipped. I think there's plenty of people around doing service industry jobs that have Bachelor's degrees, which is a shame, and it's a product of our service-based economy, but I hope that a graduate degree will provide me with a little more human capital.

MOD: Give this guy an A in his undergraduate, you said the stuff as an undergrad, there's a lot of human capital talking seminars, but that's what we've got from our side and really want to thank you 'cause that was great, that was exactly what we were looking for. I think we'll do six or eight of these from people from all kinds of different departments, and get a pretty good look at it I think. You guys have both got pretty positive experiences, it's not always that way. It's interesting, we get two positives, two negatives, one of each, and people always have something to talk about, it's like why it works, why it doesn't work, why it works for me, why it doesn't work for you. So it's a good picture, and departments can be so different. You guys were saying it's hard to figure out exactly where you're supposed to be, others say it's so rigid, I can't take anything, so it's really fun to hear the differences. Thanks a lot.

END OF SESSION

References

Allan, G. 1980. A note on interviewing spouses together. *Journal of Marriage and the Family, 42*, 205–10.

Arskey, H. 1996. Collecting data through joint interviews. *Social Research Update, 15*, 1–8.

Berger, C., & Calabrese, R. 1975. Some exploration in initial interaction and beyond: Toward a developmental theory of communication. *Human Communication Research, 1*, 99–112.

Bjornholt, M., & Farstad, G. 2012. "Am I rambling?": On the advantages of interviewing couples together. *Qualitative Research, 14*, 3–19.

Borland, T., & Amos, A. 2009. An exploratory study of the perceived impact of raising the age of cigarette purchase on young smokers in Scotland. *Public Health, 123*, 673–79.

Braun, V., & Clarke, V. 2006. Using thematic analysis in psychology. *Qualitative Research in Psychology, 3*, 77–101.

———. 2012. Thematic analysis. Cooper, H. (Ed.), *Handbook of Research Methods in Psychology* (pp. 57–71). Washington D.C.: American Psychological Association.

Charmaz, K. 2014. *Constructing Grounded Theory: A Practical Guide through Qualitative Analysis* (2nd ed.). Thousand Oaks, CA: Sage Publications.

Coenen, M., Stamm, T., Stucki, G., & Ciez, A. 2012. Individual interviews and focus groups in patients with rheumatoid arthritis: A comparison of two qualitative methods. *Quality of Life Research, 21*, 359–70.

Cronk, L., Gerkey, D., & Irons, W. 2009. Interviews as experiments: Using audience effects to examine social relationships. *Field Methods, 21*, 331–46.

Duggleby, W. 2005. What about interaction in focus group data? *Qualitative Health Research, 15*(6), 832–40.

Eggenberger, S. K., & Nelms, T. P. 2007. Family interviews as a method for family research. *Journal of Advanced Nursing, 58*, 282–92.

Eisikovits, Z., & Koren, C. 2010. Approaches to and outcomes of dyadic interview analysis. *Qualitative Health Research, 20*, 1642–55.

Galupo M., & St. John, S. 2001. Benefits of cross-sexual orientation friendships among adolescent females. *Journal of Adolescence 24*, 83–93.

Greenbaum, T. (1998), *The Handbook for Focus Group Research* (2nd ed.). Thousand Oaks, CA: Sage Publications.

Gronkjaer M., Curtis, T., Crespigny, C., & Delmar, C. 2011. Analysing group interaction in focus group research: Impact on content and the role of the moderator. *Qualitative Studies, 2*, 16–30.

Guest G., Bunce, A., & Johnson, L. 2006. How many interviews are enough? An experiment with data saturation and variability. *Field Methods, 18*, 59–82.

Halkier, B. 2010. Focus groups as social enactments: Integrating interaction and content in the analysis of focus group data. *Qualitative Research, 10*, 71–89.

Harden J., Backett-Milburn, K., Hill, M., & MacLean, A. 2010. Oh, what a tangled web we weave: Experiences of doing "multiple perspectives" research in families. *International Journal of Social Research Methodology, 13*, 441–52.

Hertz, R. 1995. Separate but simultaneous interviewing of husbands and wives: Making sense of their stories. *Qualitative Inquiry, 1*, 429–51.

Highet, G. 2003. Cannabis and smoking research: Interviewing young people in self-selected friendship pairs. *Health Education Research, 18*, 108–18.

Holmes T., Bond, L., & Byrne, C. 2012. The role of beliefs in mother-adolescent conflict: An application of the theory of planned behavior. *Current Psychology, 31*, 122–43.

Hyden, L., & Bulow P. 2003. Who's talking: Drawing conclusions from focus groups. *International Journal of Social Research Methodology, 6*, 305–21.

Jones S., Mannino, S., & Green, S. 2010. "Like me, want me, buy me, eat me": Relationship-building marketing communications in children's magazines. *Public Health Nutrition, 13*, 2111–18.

Kitzinger, J. 1994. The methodology of focus groups: The importance of interaction between research participants. *Sociology of Health & Illness, 16*, 103–21.

Koenig Kellas, J. 2005. Family ties: Communicating identity through jointly told family stories. *Communication Monographs, 72,* 365–89.

Krippendorff, K. 2012. *Content Analysis: An Introduction to Its Methodology.* Thousand Oaks, CA: Sage Publications.

Krueger, R. 1998. *Developing Questions for Focus Groups.* Thousand Oaks, CA: Sage Publications.

Krueger, R., & Casey, M. 2014. *Focus Groups: A Practical Guide for Applied Research* (5th ed.). Thousand Oaks, CA: Sage Publications.

Kvale, S., & Brinkman, S. 2008. *InterViews: Learning the Craft of Qualitative Research Interviewing.* Thousand Oaks, CA: Sage Publications.

Lehoux, P., Poland, B., & Daudelin, G. 2006. Focus group research and "the patient's view." *Social Science and Medicine, 63,* 2091–2104.

Lincoln, Y., & Guba, E. 1985. *Naturalistic Inquiry.* Thousand Oaks, CA: Sage Publications.

Mariampolski, H. 2001. *Qualitative Marketing Research.* Thousand Oaks, CA: Sage Publications.

Mayring, P. 2000. Qualitative content analysis. *Forum: Qualitative Social Research, 1*(2).

Moen, J., Antonov, K., Nilson, L., & Ring, L. 2010. Interaction between participants in focus groups with older patients and general practitioners. *Qualitative Health Research, 20,* 607–17.

McCarthy, J., Holland, J., & Gilles, V. 2003. Multiple perspectives on the "family" lives of young people: Methodological and theoretical issues in case study research. *International Journal of Social Research Methodology, 6,* 1–23.

Morantz, G., Rousseau, C., & Heymann, J. 2012. The divergent experiences of children and adults in the relocation process: Perspectives of child and parent refugee claimants in Montreal. *Journal of Refugee Studies, 25,* 71–92.

Morgan, D. L. 1993. Qualitative content analysis: A guide to paths not taken. *Qualitative Health Research, 2,* 112–21.

———. 1996. *Focus Groups as Qualitative Research* (2nd ed.). Thousand Oaks, CA: Sage Publications.

———. 2010. Reconsidering the role of interaction in analyzing and reporting focus groups. *Qualitative Health Research, 20,* 718–22.

———. 2012. Focus groups and social interaction. In J. Gubrium & J. Holstein (Eds.), *Handbook of Interview Research* (2nd ed., pp. 161–76). Thousand Oaks, CA: Sage Publications.

Morgan, D. L., Ataie, J., Carder, P., & Hoffman, K. 2013. Introducing dyadic interviews as a method for collecting qualitative data. *Qualitative Health Research, 23* (9), 1276–84.

Morgan, D. L., Eliot, S., Lowe, R. & Gorman, P. (in press). Dyadic interviews as a tool for qualitative evaluation. *American Journal of Evaluation.*

Morgan, D. L., Fellows, C., & Guevara, H. 2008. Emergent approaches to focus groups research. In S. Hesse-Biber & P. Leavy (Eds.), *Handbook of Emergent Methods* (pp. 189–206). New York: Guilford Press.

Morgan, D. L., & Lobe, B. 2011. Online focus groups. In S. Hesse-Biber (Ed.), *The Handbook of Emergent Technologies in Social Research* (pp. 199–230). Oxford: Oxford University Press.

Morgan, D. L., & Zhao, P. 1993. The doctor-caregiver relationship: Managing the care of family members with Alzheimer's disease. *Qualitative Health Research, 3,* 133–64.

Morris, S. M. 2001. Joint and individual interviewing in the context of cancer. *Qualitative Health Research, 11,* 553–67.

Myers, G. 1998. Displaying opinions: Topics and disagreement in focus groups. *Language in Society, 27,* 85–111.

———. 2007. Enabling talk: How the facilitator shapes a focus group. *Text & Talk, 27,* 79–105.

Myers, G., & Macnaghten, P. 1999. Can focus groups be analysed as talk? In R. Barbour, & J. Kitzinger (Eds.), *Developing Focus Group Research* (pp. 173–186). Thousand Oaks, CA: Sage Publications

O'Rourke, M., & Germino, B. 2000. From two perspectives to one choice: Blending couple and individual views of prostate cancer treatment selection. *Journal of Family Nursing, 6*, 231–51.

Puchta, C., & Potter, J. 2002. Manufacturing individual opinions: Market research focus groups and the discursive psychology of evaluation. *British Journal of Social Psychology, 41*, 345–63.

———. 2004. Focus group practice. Thousand Oaks, CA: Sage Publications.

Randle, M., Mackay, H., & Dudley, D. 2014. A comparison of group-based research methods. *Market & Social Research*, 22: 22–35.

Reczek, C. 2014. Conducting a multi-family member interview study. *Family Process, 53*, 318–35.

Rubin, H. J., & Rubin I. 2011. *Qualitative Interviewing: The Art of Hearing Data* (3rd ed.). Thousand Oaks, CA: Sage Publications.

Seale, C., Charteris-Black, J., Dumelow, C., Locok, L., & Ziebland, S. 2008. The effect of joint interviewing on the performance of gender. *Field Methods, 20*, 107–28.

Spradley, J. P. 1979. *The Ethnographic Interview*. Fort Worth: Holt, Rinehart and Winston.

Starkweather, S. 2012. Telling family stories: Collaborative storytelling, taking precedence, and giving precedence in family group interviews with Americans in Singapore. *Area, 43*, 289–95.

Strauss, A., & Corbin, J. 1998. *Basics of Qualitative Research* (2nd ed.). Thousand Oaks, CA: Sage Publications.

Vaismoradi, M., Turunen, H., & Bondas, T. 2013. Content analysis and thematic analysis: Implications for conducting a qualitative descriptive study. *Nursing and Health Sciences, 15*, 398–405.

Valentine, G. 1999. Doing housework research: Interviewing couples together and apart. *Area, 31*, 67–74.

Wang, C., & Burris, M. A. 1997. Photovoice: Concept, methodology, and use for participatory needs assessment. *Health Education & Behavior, 24*, 369–87.

Wilkinson, S. 1998a. Focus groups in feminist research: Power, interaction and the co-construction of meaning. *Women's Studies International Forum, 21*, 111–25.

———. 1998b. Focus groups in health research: Exploring the meanings of health and illness. *Journal of Health Psychology, 33*, 329–48.

Index

About the Author

David L. Morgan is a professor in the Department of Sociology at Portland State University. He was instrumental in bringing the use of focus groups to social science research and is also one of the leading figures in the use of mixed methods. His books include *Focus Groups as Qualitative Research*, five volumes of the *Focus Group Kit*, and *Integrating Qualitative and Quantitative Methods*.

71531408R00069

Made in the USA
San Bernardino, CA
16 March 2018